Polarizing language is a device used to cover up lies, deceit and all kinds of deceptions. People should be mindful of this.

RULES
for
PUBLIC DISCOURSE

**Holding Lawmakers
Accountable for
False Statements,
Misrepresentations and
Unsubstantiated Claims**

A satire on Politics in America

By Charles Hoppins

Published by Western Research Press
A division of Western Research Institute, Inc.
P.O. Box 45061
Boise ID 83711-5061

For information write:
Western Research Press
P.O. Box 17192
Lost Angeles CA 90017

Telephone number: (208) 703-5709
Email address: westernresearach@earthlink.net.
Web Site http://wrii.org (Some browsers such as Google Chrome try to reroute this URL)
Alternative URL http://wikiwacky.net/wrii

Print edition:
ISBN-10: 1-882567-51-X
ISBN-13: 978-1-882567-51-5

98765

This book is dedicated to Pollyanna
(Good things really do happen even in politics)

Nimis quidpiam serio non aspice

PREFACE

Voters across the United States are nearly equally divided about many major issues such as abortion, gay marriage, the definition of truth, gun control, civil rights and many other subjects. It doesn't matter what you believe about many things, it is likely that close to half the population will agree with you and close to half will disagree with you. In some cases such as abortion and gun control, the range is probably closer to 60 to 40 percent. In cases like gay rights, sodomy and gay marriage, it is probably closer to 50 percent. However, the attitude about gay marriage seems to be changing with more people favoring it.

In the matter of the definition of truth, informal surveys by Western Research Institute, Inc., indicate that close to 60 percent believe that truth is objective while close to 40 percent of the population believe that truth is relative. What you believe about the definition of truth often colors your belief about other things.

FRUSTATION

Many people are frustrated in trying to resolve issues with people who hold different views. This is especially true when the other party or parties are dishonest and lack integrity. People are frustrated by blatant misstatements by members of the U.S. Congress and by candidates for public office who engage in clichés, innuendoes, party-line prattle, false statements and rhetoric that has no substance.

Many lawmakers and candidates for public office are guilty of violating the Rules for Public Discourse. They have:

- Made unsubstantiated claims.
- Evaded questions.
- Misrepresented opponents positions.
- Made statements that were false.
- Were dishonest in advertisements.

There are individuals, corporations, foundations and PACs, flush with money, who use their financial resources to sway public opinion, win elections and influence members of Congress. They can be identified by their wholesale violation of the Rules for Public Discourse.[1]

While most journalists and news media are honest and have integrity and try to be fair and balanced in the way they report the news, there are exceptions, especially in the broadcast media. They too can be identified by the way they violate the Rules for Public Discourse

Add to this mix are the power brokers, the political pundits the analysts, the consultants and contributors, many of whom also violate the Rules for Public Discourse. Rules for Public Discourse are proposed to identify dishonesty and a Patriot Pledge is proposed to hold lawmakers and political candidates accountable for their actions

It needs to be stressed that the author is really not delusional in proposing rules such as these and a Patriot Pledge in times such as these. This book is born out of desperation to see a crack of moderation in the current climate of hostility, hyperbole and polarizing language.

In response this book is much about the science of logic, that part of philosophy of which most of academia are in agreement

So to counter those who poo poo the notion of enforcing the Rules for Public Discourse and the Patriot Pledge on a broad scale, we have instituted the Tea Party Police who will gather evidence on those guilty of violating the Rules and the Pledge and hand them over to the court of public opinion. Those who wish to join the Tea Party Police and political candidates and lawmakers who wish to make the Patriot Pledge may do so by going to wrii.org (The full URL is wikiwacky.net/wrii).

Logic is the division of philosophy that deals with right reason, identification of false statements and faulty arguments. The Rules for Public Discourse are formulated on formal logic and to question them is to question the principles of formal logic.

THE PATRIOT PLEDGE

The Patriot Pledge is the pledge lawmakers and political candidates should be required to take to determine their worthiness for public office. The Patriot Pledge replaces the pledge lawmakers make to Grover Norquist. The two are not always compatible.

The Patriot Pledge states:

I pledge allegiance to the United States of America. I further pledge:

My first priority shall be to do what is in the best interests of my country.

My second priority shall be to do what is in the best interests of my state and my constituents.

And only after the first two priorities are met shall I do what is in my own best interests and the best interests of those to whom I am beholden.

TABLE OF CONTENTS

APPENDIXES

.

INTRODUCTION

It is a fact that many if not most politicians and lawmakers in state and national offices are dishonest in that they at certain times lie in order to achieve their objectives. And it is a fact that some politicians and some state and national officeholders consistently lie and promote objectives and laws that are against the public interest.

Did you know that there are certain principles and rules that when applied to dishonest statements can immediately identify them as lies. In addition there are rules which when applied to all statements can identify those that are problematic. These principles and rules can thus identify people that are lying by the very nature of what they say.

Identifying them will not make people who are making dishonest statements or lying stop making them. Some believe that if you make a false statement often enough there will be people who will believe it. The only way to deal with this genre of lawmakers is to vote them out of office. But building a case of dishonesty may be difficult. Many people are not interested in the truth or for that matter what makes a thing or statement true.

It is easy to forget the acrimonious conduct of the 112th Congress in 2011 and 2012 that shocked the nation. It had Republicans, Democrats and political pundits making accusations of dishonesty and misrepresentations. There seemed to be a disconnect in positions advanced by each side with no way to resolve the dilemma.

That was small potatoes compared to the government shutdown in October 2013. Republicans launched a full-scale attack on the Affordable Care Act in an effort to get it defunded or at least delayed a year. The shutdown marked a new level of intransigence on the part of both sides. Polls showed disapproval ratings for Republicans soared past 70 percent and soared past 50 percent for Democrats.

This book goes to great lengths in exploring opposing belief systems and reasons why it is so difficult for some people in and out of Congress to come to an understanding of certain issues and reach agreement on anything. It has to do with communication. People in general, especially those in public office, seem to be just not interested in dialogue where two or more people engage in an unbiased discussion of issues.

In a way it is understandable. If somebody disagrees with someone about a serious matter such as money, that someone tends to get upset. Passions can run high. This is the predicament of Congress. Members are in disagreement on fundamental questions: the scope of government, social programs, taxes and spending, and the role the government should play in regulating business.

Disagreement is one thing, but the degree of hostility that one faction of one party was able to engender marked a new benchmark in American politics. To further complicate matters were the extreme position some Tea Party supporters and their financial backers took in threatening lawmakers who strayed from their ideology.

PARTY BASES

The standoff had many in the traditional base of the Republican Party calling for moderation and displayed what some pundits said were the loss of influence that business and financial interests traditional wielded.

To complicate matters were the still in play so-called traditional bases of the Republican and Democratic parties, which in effect hold their candidates hostage to far right and far left positions and to which the respective candidates for public office must pander. Holding these positions are people who are manipulated by big business and big labor and other conservative and liberal organizations pushing a particular agenda.

Many Republicans and many Democrats are unreasonable in their positions. One cannot maintain an unreasonable position without making false statements, assertions lacking in proof, and flawed arguments.[1]

Preliminary results of polls being conducted by the author, indicate there is an enormous gap in the beliefs of various members of the general public as to how they perceive what is going on in Washington, what is real, what is not, what is true, what is false and the nature of reality and of truth itself.[2]

The public discourse of lawmakers is directed at their constituents. What they say is often not what people hear. Or rather what one person hears is often different from what another person hears. What a person believes shapes his or her perception of reality and their understanding of what is said..

People, raised in different circumstances with opposing beliefs, are set in their ways. Everybody has their own agenda, their own special set of beliefs, their own ethnic biases, their own problems and their own needs. They do not have (or won't take) time to listen to other points of view. They are preoccupied with themselves and their immediate needs. Like Henry David Thoreau said, "Most people live lives of quiet desperation."

Sometimes in serious matters, communicating their agenda and their beliefs results in miscommunication. Often people do not realize they are not communicating. For most people, their mind is made up and they don't reflect on the possibility that some of their views might be in error. Plato's comment that "the unexamined life is not worth living" gets little traction in today's America.

As Mortimer Adler said in a speech in 1961, "It is almost impossible for any of us to use any words that are understood by other people in exactly the sense in which we use them.

"Even the most careful and precise use of language, which is difficult sometimes to accomplish, leaves the result incomplete, inadequate, and, often worse than that, something that is moving in the wrong direction..."[3]

So, it is likely then, that some statements between lawmakers themselves, between lawmakers and their constituents and among constituents themselves may not be accurate. This is always a possibility.

Throw into this mix dishonest assertions, inaccurate statements and false claims by lawmakers, power brokers, political pundits and others, and people are going to be misled and believe things that are not true.

In an effort to hold public officials accountable for what they say for public consumption, there is created in this book Rules for Public Discourse. These are laid out in Chapter VII and explained in Chapter IX. Rules for Public Discourse can help reign in the rhetoric and help the voting public spot false statements and unsubstantiated claims.

To further meaningful communication between two or more people, among lawmakers themselves, between them and their constituents and among their constituents themselves, there is created in this book Precepts of Dialogue. These are the subject of the next to last chapter.

In order to promote civility and good manners there is listed some rules of civility in Chapter XV, "Other Rules."

And in order to help people discern what is true and what is false about many things, and what to believe and not to believe about all things, there is listed at the end of Chapter XVI some Precepts of Discernment.

CHAPTER I
IS WASHINGTON BROKEN?

President Barack Obama said in his 2012 State of the Union address that "Washington is broken."

What is "Washington" and what constitutes "broken"? Washington is a broad term used loosely to refer to the three branches of the U.S. government and the cadre of lobbyists, journalists, pundits and politicians who inhabit the U.S. capital, but often more particularly to Congress, the lawmaking body of government, which consists of the U.S. Senate and the U.S. House of Representatives. "Broken" is the term employed to describe the acrimonious conduct of lawmakers in each body of the Congress since election of President Obama.

There are many reasons that result in acrimonious conduct. They can generally be boiled down to reprehensible behavior by many members of each party, which includes:

- Lack of civility
- Lack of integrity
- Dishonesty
- Ignorance
- Misguided conduct
- Misplaced priorities
- Inability or unwillingness to communicate

There is a theory espoused in this book that the inability or unwillingness to communicate is behind much of this acrimony. Each side is frustrated because the other side is either not able or is unwilling to understand or accept the position of the other side and vice versa. To communicate and create dialogue each side must reign in the rhetoric and actually seek out strengths in the positions of their opponents.

To complicate matters there are lawmakers who actually create dissension as a means of obstructing resolutions on certain issues.

Practically speaking, reigning in the rhetoric is not likely to happen. Constructive dialogue between the two sides is also unlikely. The only way change will happen is through the ballot box. The only way it will happen through the ballot box is if voters hone in on those who abide by the Rules for Public Discourse.

PRIORITIES

In the matter of priorities, each member of Congress should do firstly what is in the best interests of the country; do secondly what is in the best interests of their state and the people they represent; and only after the first two priorities have been met, do what is in their own and their family's best interest, and only then to special interests to which they are beholden.

Unfortunately, judging by their actions, many members of Congress put their own best interests and the interest of their party first and the best interests of their country last and in so doing they end up fighting among themselves for the spoils of government.

Even then, there should be productive efforts to achieve what is best for the country. Civil men and women should be able to sit down together and work out their differences. The reasons they can't is because of intransigence based on the above.

There are many rules of conduct by which people can be held accountable. Many professions have enacted rules or codes which govern their members.[1] In addition there are general rules such as rules of civility.[2] There are precepts of dialogue.[3] There are rules which govern debate.[4] There are rules which govern argument.[5] There are many other sets of rules for many other situations. And there are rules for public discourse which are the subject of this book.

Unfortunately there is no established authority, which recognizes these rules and which, when applied to Congress, can hold accountable those who violate them except the people. The ultimate authority is left to the population in general and the electorate, which voted the members of Congress into office.

To establish standards in the minds of people is the purpose of the succeeding chapters of this book. Any member of Congress (or member of any legislative body, for that matter) who does not abide by these standards is either lacking in integrity and is dishonest, or is ignorant or misguided or a combination thereof.

Each individual has basic beliefs that are common to everybody. Some of these beliefs are formed as a result of experience. Some are formed as a result of education. Collectively they form a common sense which govern the actions of each individual. The rules expounded here are a part of common sense and will be recognized as such by people who are introduced to them.

There are lawmakers in Congress who have integrity and there are lawmakers in Congress who lack integrity. They can generally be identified by their public statements and how they vote, especially in committee.

The stakes are so high and the competition so intense that there is a tendency among some senators and representatives to believe that the end justifies the means. A person gets elected to Congress and immediately has all this wealth at his fingertips. The money is floating around everywhere and it's so easy to reach out and grab some that the temptation to do so is irresistible. And those that do so lack integrity. They do it with earmarks, they do it with special interest legislation, tax breaks and loopholes, padded office expenses and accounts, entertainment and junkets paid for by lobbyists and various other ingenuous activity that is hidden from public view.

INSIDER TRADING

Prior to 2012, one third of the Senate and one half the House actively traded in the stock market using information gained in the various activities of Congress to gain a leg up on other traders. Lawmakers finally put an end to this practice in 2012.[6]

The tendency is to believe the well will never dry up. Lawmakers in the past have been so generous with wages, benefits, programs and tax breaks that it has created an overbalance of spending versus revenue.

There is plenty of money available to solve the debt crisis. What is lacking is political will. The statement that "Washington is broken"—more specifically that "the U.S. Congress is dysfunctional"—assumes that this is the correct representation of the way things are. In deference to House Republicans, there is another view that the bitter acrimony and brinkmanship of the 112th Congress is the way a democracy is supposed to function. The stakes are high for everybody concerned. And it is mostly about money: who gets what slice of the pie from the economy and from the government.

NO EASY ANSWER

The answer to the above question is not easy. There are those who maintain that bringing this kind of pressure is necessary to rein in the spendthrift ways of Congress and solve the debt crisis. Our purpose here is not to answer this question. Our purpose here is one of discernment—to provide tools to better determine which lawmakers have integrity and which lawmakers do not have integrity.

The stakes in this drama are incredibly high. It is about the future of the United States, which is at stake. And the integrity of those who are putting the future of this country at stake over who gets what slice of the economic pie is a valid question. False statements and misrepresentations are not only not helpful, but contribute to the obfuscation of the issues and are highly detrimental to any constructive solution to the problems that are faced.

FISCAL RESPONSIBILITY

Fiscal responsibility—the management of finances—determines the health of a nation, the health of political subdivisions within it and the financial health of the individuals and families that make it up. When the management of financial affairs fails, the social fabric of the entity involved deteriorates. People and businesses that spend more money than they receive in revenue are bound to eventually fail.

The good management of its financial affairs and lack of wholesale corruption was a major factor in what made the United States a great nation. The bad management of financial affairs and corruption in government is what has made many countries, especially dictatorships, poor or outright failures. In addition it is a national security issue. Having a surplus instead of a debt to deal with gives China a tremendous advantage over the United States. In the last decade the U.S. has fallen prey to extremely bad management.

CHAPTER II
WHAT IS INTEGRITY

A man or woman is said to have integrity if he or she is polite, honest, caring, and has the right priorities. That means he or she abides by the rules of civility, the rules for public discourse, basic tenets of morality and is willing to brace others who do not.

But the key to integrity is having the right priorities. Presidents, lawmakers and people in government can serve themselves or they can serve their country. The way the American political system functions is an invitation to corruption. Many are seduced by it and try to serve two masters. Even those, whose integrity is beyond question, are under constant assault.

It is said that power corrupts and absolute power corrupts absolutely. For even the most honorable some corruption seems likely. Honest men are prone to lie and cheat for power... and money. Those seeking office and those in office must constantly chase contributions to gain or stay in office. They become beholden to special interests. The people from whom members of Congress must solicit funds are often unscrupulous and seeking favors that are in direct opposition to the public interest.

Into this unholy mix is the temptation of members of Congress to say and do what is expedient, not what is right, true or correct. Thus we have men and women in Congress and pundits in the press making statements that cannot be proven or are outright false and making arguments that are fallacious. They attack the person instead of the argument. They misrepresent opposing points of view. They have lost or have never had integrity.

INTEGRITY

Not all members of Congress and people in government have lost their integrity. By applying the Rules, which follow, we can identify those in Congress and those in the media who do not have integrity and those who do have integrity.

In the halcyon days after World War II, colleges and universities were filled with returning veterans on the GI Bill. The transfer from wartime to peacetime went fairly smoothly. Dwight D. Eisenhower followed Harry Truman in the presidency and signed the legislation establishing the Interstate Highway system. Construction began in the latter years of his presidency and the nation's highways went from two lanes to freeways with 10 lanes in just a few years..

John F. Kennedy followed Eisenhower in the presidency in 1960. In his inaugural address, he asked Americans to "…ask what you can do for your country." And many Americans did. Americans in general are willing to sacrifice for their country. However now, few people are asking. Instead, people are asking "…what their country can do for them."

As we have noted, the key to integrity is having the right priorities. And the right priority is putting the best interest of the country first. It is in the public's interest that the best interest of the country outweighs all other considerations.

There may be disagreement about what is in the best interest of the country. And this is often what all the debate is about. And it is in debate that the best interest of the country is often determined...or not determined. Often in debate, lawmakers seek to justify the protection of some special interest or their advocacy of certain positions that are, in fact, contrary to the best interests of the county.

It may be that often the best interest of the country is not obvious and opposing points of view are legitimate subjects for discussion. On the other hand there are scenarios in which lawmakers seek to maintain unreasonable positions on what is best for the country.

UNREASONABLE POSITIONS

An example is the polarization evidenced by extreme positions within each party. These extreme positions are generally unreasonable and are not in the best interests of the country. [1]

The one thing about unreasonable positions is they cannot be justified by established facts and legitimate arguments. Lawmakers often hold to unreasonable positions and in order to do so they must resort to false claims and unjustified assertions. Lawmakers who resort to false statements, knowing they are false, and unsubstantiated claims have lost, or never had, integrity. Thus we may see some lawmakers belittling the importance of always making statements that are true and claims that are substantiated.

It is by using rules for public discourse and certain investigative procedures that false statements, misrepresentations, unsubstantiated claims and fallacious arguments, and those who make them, can be identified. Lawmakers so identified as consistent violators of these rules are not honest and lack integrity and need to be publicly exposed and excoriated. Candidates and lawmakers need to realize that consistent violation of the Rules will make them ineligible for public office.

There are many things that can be debated about what is in the best interest of the country. The one thing that stands out above all others is resolution of the deficit and the astronomical debt. It is a crisis that has potentially disastrous consequences. Continued borrowing of huge sums could conceivably reach the point where it would create a Greek-like scenario and break the country. It is utterly irresponsible for the current Congress to let selfish interests stand in the way of a solution. Resolving the debt crisis would go a long way toward resolving other problems facing the country, like unemployment and economic growth.

CHAPTER III
THE CURRENT CLIMATE

Congress' approval rating is the lowest it has ever been, around nine percent as of this writing, which is pretty bad. Veteran observers of the political scene in Washington say they have never seen the degree of intransigent behavior present in the Congress that so prevents resolution of the current fiscal crisis. By intransigent behavior is meant the animosity and mean spirited attacks on holders of opposing positions. Those doing so are often dishonest in what they say.
.

It is a game of brinkmanship, of high-stakes, no limit, poker. Whatever the makeup, members of the House Republican Caucus has pretty much paralyzed the legislative process.

There are two factors that pretty much governed the political climate in Washington in recent years. One factor was the Tea Party. The other factor consisted of members of the Republican Party that had signed the no-new-tax pledge dictated by Grover Norquest.[1] Both factors contributed to the brinkmanship that prevailed in the U.S. House of Representatives.

The Congress is to an extent governed (some would say "held hostage") by the Tea Party. And it is the Tea Party which has much to do with the political climate in Washington. So what and who is the Tea Party?

The term "tea party" is applied to groups of people who hold certain views and to all the groups collectively. There are possibly thousands of such groups with memberships running from two people to hundreds of people. There does not appear to be any centralized apparatus that represents all of them. The Tea Party has also been characterized as "a movement" "a growing state of mind" and as an "antiparty." [2]

The U.S. House of Representatives is made up of 435 members. Of these 242 are Republicans and 193 are Democrats. At the end of the 2012, the Tea Party Caucus in the House consisted of 62 representatives. There were four members in the Senate. The caucus was created and is chaired by Michele Bachman.[3]

Norquist at the end of the year 2011 boasted that 238 House members and 41 senators had taken his "taxpayer protection pledge, which asks all candidates for federal and state office to commit themselves in writing to oppose all tax increases. Of these there were two Democratic House members and one Democratic senator[4]. There were six House Republicans and seven Republican senators who did not sign the pledge.[5]

The Tea Party had its earliest beginnings under the Bush administration with small groups of Republicans coalescing to promote conservative principles. It blossomed out in 2009 as a reaction to policies of the Obama administration, particularly health care legislation and has energized the Republican base. While there are now many disparate groups of tea partiers, all are pretty much in agreement on some basic tenets such as:

- Limited federal government
- Strengthening individual freedoms
- Reducing taxes (no new taxes)
- Reducing spending.
- Balancing the budget

- Free market economics
- Less regulation
- Repeal of health care law

On the surface, these positions are not all that radical. With the exception of the health care law, these are positions over which Democrats and Republicans have been quarreling for more than a century—the size of government, individual rights and freedoms, the role of the states versus the federal government, taxes and spending, and the role the government should play in regulating business.

What is radical are the tactics used to enforce Tea Party positions on taxes, spending and government regulation. The 2010 election results saw House Republicans gain 63 new seats, most with the help of the tea party. The new members lost little time in helping to put in place new rules that bound Republicans in the House to major changes in the way the House did business and left little room for compromise.

The position of the Republicans, about which they were intransigent, was that no new legislation involving taxes would increase revenue and all efforts to decrease the deficit must come from a reduction in federal spending.

This conflicted with the Democrats who wanted to reduce the deficit by a combination of new revenue involving taxes and a reduction in federal spending.

Republicans refused to raise the debt ceiling, which would have shut down most of the functions of the federal government, unless the Democrats agreed to substantial cuts to spending, which they finally did at the last moment.

CHAPTER IV
THE PLAYERS

There were many players that stood out during the first year of the 112th Congress including President Obama in the Executive Branch, the leaders in Congress, eight Republican presidential candidates and the host of journalists, analysts, consultants, pundits and power brokers.

In the Senate were Harry Reid and Mitch McConnell. In the House were Speaker John Boehner and majority and minority leaders Eric Cantor and Nancy Pelosi.

The presidential contenders were Mitt Romney, Newt Gingrich, Ron Paul, Rick Santorum, Rick Perry, Michele Bachmann, Jon Huntsman and Herman Cain. By the end of January 2012 their number had been paired down to Romney, Gingrich, Paul and Santorum.

Sarah Palin, Donald Trump and Mike Huckabee made a lot of noise during much of the year. Also making their presence felt were the news Web sites and bloggers on the Internet, and on radio, the unofficial spokesman for the Republican Party, Rush Limbaugh.

Taking center stage was the drama of brinkmanship in the House and the caustic tone of the Republican presidential debates. It all promised that the campaigns leading up to the general election in November would be one of the most expensive and interesting spectacles in recent memory.

We are mainly interested here, not in what everybody had to say, but whether the particular statements that were made violated one or more rules for public discourse. It may be that one or more of the players mentioned above had the good sense to limit their rhetoric to the bounds proscribed by the Rules for Public Discourse. We are only attributing violations to those that we have documented. This, of course, does not mean that because we have no documentation on a particular person, he or she has not made any violations.

In the House, there was a lot said by Boehner and Cantor and by Senators Reid and McConnell and by many other members of Congress. There were many violations of Rules for Public Discourse.

We are interested in the 100 senators and 435 representatives, members of the media, the pundits, the power brokers and the candidates for the Republican nomination for president. They have all had a part in the drama of the Congress and candidates that has played out in the media. It has been a constant item in the news and one of the main subjects of pundits, political consultants, and discussion panels on the networks, cable channels and radio stations.

Romney, Gingrich, Paul, Santorum, Perry and Bachman ended 2011 blasting each other in an effort to win the Iowa caucuses. They too, all violated Rules for Public Discourse.

CHAPTER V
PRACTICE OF DECEPTION

Much of the information we are daily confronted with is false. Discerning what is true from what is false is a function of philosophy. Philosophy provides certain tools to do this. We will be discussing them in the succeeding chapters.

The main area of philosophy that is concerned with right reason and discernment is logic. The main division of logic that is concerned with discernment is the fallacies. Knowledge of the fallacies enables us to spot an invalid argument and thereby discern what may be a false statement.

Western philosophy had its beginnings in ancient Greece. In the fifth and fourth centuries B.C., when philosophy was reaching its zenith in Greece, there were itinerant teachers (philosophy professors) who developed clever arguments to sway their listeners to any point of view. They were looked down upon and disparaged by the greatest of the Greek philosophers, Socrates, Plato, Aristotle, and others. Aristotle wrote a treatise on fallacies to refute their arguments.[1]

These itinerant teachers became known as "sophists," from which we derive the word sophism. A sophism is defined as a fallacious argument. A fallacious argument or fallacy is defined as an argument that at first appears to be valid, but upon closer examination turns out to be invalid.

To understand this we need to understand what an argument is and of what an argument consists. An argument within the discipline of logic is an inference. An inference is a conclusion drawn from one or more premises. A premise is a statement used in an argument from which a conclusion is drawn.

Premises and conclusions can be true or false. An argument is said not to be true or false, but valid or invalid, depending on whether or not the inference was correctly made. The truth or falsity of a conclusion is determined by the truth or falsity of the premises and by whether an argument is valid or invalid.

RULES OF LOGIC

The rules of logic, which determine the validity of an argument, are too extensive to be treated here. One does not need to master them to spot an invalid argument. But one should be aware that they exist.

The fallacies provide us with examples of how these rules are violated as well as other ways we can be deceived. Textbooks on logic will usually list the different classifications and many examples. And there are many sites on the Internet that cover them.[2]

Deliberate deception is found in all kinds of advertising including ads placed by political parties and advocates of political issues. There is a generally accepted standard that disdains those who deliberately seek to deceive people into believing things that are not true.

As noted before we have formulated the relevant principles of logic into the Rules for Public Discourse. As will be seen in Chapter IX, "Explanation of Rules," most of the Rules have their underpinnings in one or more fallacies.

There are many public figures who have been guilty of violating the Rules for Public Discourse and one or more fallacies. We have listed many of them in the previous chapter.

EGREGIOUS VIOLATIONS

Included among these were a number who have crossed way over the line in making false statements and need to be called out. So far we have documented egregious violations by Donald Trump, Sarah Palin, Michele Bachmann, Mike Huckabee, and Rush Limbaugh. There are many more that need to be documented.

The thing of it is, it is so unnecessary. With the exceptions of Donald Trump. who aggressively pursued the "birther" argument; Mike Huckabee, who later recanted; and Rush Limbaugh, who is a consistent violator of the Rules; Michele Bachmann and many others could have made the same pronouncements without violating any of the rules for public discourse. It's as if they didn't understand what truth is or didn't know what makes a thing true or really didn't care (which is hard to imagine).

The rules for public discourse also bestow rights on lawmakers and others who speak out. People (including lawmakers) have a right to make a statement and to change or retract it. Perhaps Mike Huckabee restored some of his credibility in disavowing his statement that Obama grew up in Kenya.[3]

Mike Huckabee said on Fox News that President Obama grew up in Kenya. It may be argued that Huckabee was ignorant of where Obama grew up, which is almost as bad.

"BIRTHER ARGUMENTS"

Another controversy that arose during the 2012 Republican primary campaign were the "birther" arguments that Obama was not born in the United States, a position forcefully pursued by Donald Trump and supported for a time by Fox News. This was an egregious violation of the Third Rule for Public Discourse which says, *Thou shalt not make unsubstantiated claims.* Trump and others making similar claims were justifiably excoriated by various members of the press in news articles and broadcast journalists.

Probably the most consistent violator of the Rules for Public Discourse was Michele Bachmann. She refused to respond to questions. . She repeatedly refused to address an issue by talking about a totally different subject, which is the violation of the Second Rule for Public Discourse. She consistently made unsubstantiated claims and made false statements, violations of Rules Three and Four. She also violated many of the other Rules.

PEOPLE NOT STUPID

People are not stupid. They see through these ruses. This may be one of the reasons she was at the bottom of the Republican field and dropped out of the running.

Sarah Palin, who was chosen by Sen. John McCain to be his vice presidential running mate in the 2008 presidential election campaign, had trouble keeping her facts straight. Perhaps her most dishonest misrepresentation as a Republican power broker was her coining of the phrase "death panel" in regard to Obama's health care legislation. This also spawned a television advertisement that showed an old woman struggling in a wheel chair being wheeled down a path and pushed over a cliff.

Palin said on Facebook in August of 2009, "…my parents and my baby with Down Syndrome will have to stand in front of Obama's 'death panel' so his bureaucrats can decide based on a subjective judgment of their 'level of productivity in society,' whether they are worthy of health care." The remark has occasioned excoriation in the media.

CHAPTER VI
REIGNING IN RHETORIC

The U.S. has faced many crises, all, or nearly all, of which this country—the president and the Congress, Democrats and Republicans—have been able to resolve. Whether the continuing crisis involving the deficit and the debt will be resolved should be on everybody's mind.

The objective of Rules for Public Discourse is to reign in the rhetoric. Making claims that are not factual or accurate is not helpful to resolving conflict and reaching solutions to problems. They are in fact counter-productive and may even be insurmountable obstacles to reaching agreements.

To hold lawmakers accountable, there needs to be established some criteria of behavior in addition to the rules Congress has put in place to punish unethical behavior. There needs to be rules governing what is acceptable and what is not acceptable in what is said for public consumption.

The Rules for Public Discourse set forth in this treatise are an attempt to establish some basic criteria for what is acceptable and what is not acceptable in statements made by lawmakers and others for public consumption.

While expounding on the Rules for Public Discourse is the primary thrust of this book, there are a number of other rules, that people have put in place to govern conduct that should be noted to reinforce the introduction of Rules for Public Discourse.

As mentioned in Chapter I, some of them are:[1]

- Rules for specific professions
- Precepts of dialogue
- Rules of civility
- Rules of debate
- Rules for argument

Each set of rules has a different objective. Out of all these there are two sets of rules which can help in holding lawmakers accountable for what they accomplish or don't accomplish. They are Rules of Civility and Precepts of Dialogue. The Rules of Civility are about etiquette and good manners. The Precepts of Dialogue are about meaningful communication which goes beyond ordinary discourse. In order to avoid confusion, we will save discussing the Rules of Civility and Precepts of Dialogue until the next-to-last chapters.

There is much written on dialogue, debate, rhetoric and argumentation, all of which are aspects of communication, and all of which have application to rules for public discourse. It will be helpful to define the terms used to identify these various forms of communication.

Communication is a broad term encompassing body language, nuances and other forms of expression by which we exchange various forms of data. Here we are concerned only with verbal or written communication, the use of language, so to speak.

Definitions of these terms are:

Discourse is *formal discussion of a subject.*

Public Discourse is *a statement made for consumption by the general public.*

Dialogue is *constructive discourse between two or more people about a specific subject.*

Meaningful Communication as used in this text is *a special kind of discourse in which the Precepts of Dialogue are observed.*

Rhetoric is *the art or study of using language effectively and persuasively.*

Debate is *a contest of persuasion between two or more people discussing opposing points of view.*

Argument has a number of definitions within the context of communication. The one used here is *a discussion of different points of view.* Thus it is distinguished from an **argument in formal logic**, which is *the setting out of an inference by which a conclusion is drawn from one or more premises.*

The Precepts of Dialogue mentioned above are the positive side of the Rules for Public Discourse. Thus the Precepts of Dialogue are about rights of the communicator, while Rules for Public Discourse are more about commandments—what the communicator is forbidden to do.

CHAPTER VII
RULES FOR
PUBLIC DISCOURSE

We have a singular purpose here. That is to establish rules for public discourse to hold lawmakers accountable for what they say for public consumption. It is incumbent upon everyone seeking integrity in government to understand these rules and see that they are enforced.

I. Thou shalt not prevent anyone from speaking out.

Everybody has the right to be heard, to make a statement and to change or retract it.

II. Thou shalt not evade a question by addressing another issue or by responding to a question with a question.

Respond to another person by addressing the issue raised by that person

III. Thou shalt not make unsubstantiated claims.

Any person making a categorical statement, asserting one or more facts has the obligation to provide proof of the truth or validity of the facts asserted.

IV. Thou shalt not make a false statement or advance a false position.

Everybody has the obligation to tell the truth.

V. Thou shalt not deliberately misrepresent any point of view.

Everybody has the obligation to understand an opposing point of view and to represent it correctly.

VI. Thou shalt acknowledge opposition statements.

Any person has a right to disagree with the position(s) and/or statement(s) of any other person.

VII. Thou shalt distinguish between a person and the statement or argument of that person.

All parties have the obligation to distinguish between a person and the position and/or statements of that person.

VIII. Thou shalt not impute.

No one has the right to impute to another person beliefs, knowledge, ignorance, feelings, thoughts, understanding, intentions, positions or any other thing.

X. Thou shalt not use a negative universal statement in an assertion or in an argument.

> Negative universal statements are such that they generally cannot be proven and therefore cannot legitimately be made.

X. Thou shalt not use fallacious or illogical arguments.

> Fallacious arguments cannot legitimately be made.

All of these Rules have ramifications and some are not as simple as they appear to be on the surface. Following in the Chapter IX is an explanation of each of these Rules and why it is important that they be adhered to.

But first understanding the philosophical principles behind the establishment of these Rules will be helpful in understanding the way they are formulated. Thus, the role of philosophy is the subject of the next chapter.

CHAPTER VIII
THE ROLE OF PHILOSOPHY

Philosophy does not appear to hold the attraction for people it once held in prior centuries. Hence, the understanding of philosophical subjects and principles by the general public is limited. Books about philosophy do not generally reach best seller lists. Relatively few college students major in philosophy. Probably most of the general public is unaware of what the subject of philosophy consists.[1]

There are two philosophical principles, the understanding of which are critical to the production of constructive results in the use of the Rules and Precepts laid down in this book. Before dwelling on these, a little background is in order.

There are many systems of philosophy. The most wellknown systems are those constructed by Plato and Aristotle. Both built on systems promulgated by earlier Greek philosophers. We will use the term "belief system" to denote the totality of positions held by a particular philosopher or philosophy. A "belief system" can also apply to the totality of an individual's conscious and subconscious beliefs. A position is a person's point of view on a particular issue.

And so down through the ages each succeeding generation of philosophers built succeeding belief systems by making certain alterations to the systems of their predecessors. Theoretically any system of philosophy must be built on certain basic principles, assumptions or positions. And the totality of positions of any belief system can theoretically be logically traced back to certain principles, assumptions or positions on which a particular philosophical belief system is based.

Aristotle established the principle of contradiction as the first principle on which his philosophical belief system is based. Generally, succeeding generations of philosophers accepted this first principle and built their philosophical belief systems accordingly.

Rene Descartes in the 17th Century built his philosophical belief system on his famous dictum, "cogito ergo sum," *I think, therefore I am*. This split succeeding philosophical thinking into two parts, idealism and realism. Still, he accepted the principle of contradiction as a valid principle as did nearly all the philosophers succeeding him—until the 20th century.

As time progressed, philosophical belief systems fragmented and multiplied. Now the number of philosophical belief systems stands in a certain direct ratio to the number of professional philosophers.

The two philosophical principles that are critical to dialogue are the principle of contradiction and the distinction between exterior reality and interior reality.

> The principle of contradiction states: **A thing cannot be.. and not be.. at the same time and in the same respect.**

USING THE PRINCIPLE OF CONTRADICTION

There are a number of ways the principle of contradiction can be used. By using the principle of contradiction, you can prove a negative statement to be false and you can prove many beliefs and positions to be false. A negative statement is such that it generally cannot be proven. But it can be proven to be false by proving a statement that contradicts it. This is discussed more fully in Chapter XII, "The Nature of Proof."

In logic, propositions (statements) and terms are divided into particular and universal and positive and negative. Universal statements can be likened to and have the same sense as general statements. A positive universal (term or statement) is all inclusive as in "all men" and "all automobiles are self-propelled." A negative universal is all exclusive as in "no man" or "no man is an island." Likewise there are particular positive terms or statements as in "that man" and "some men are great." Particular negative terms or statements would be "not that man" and "some men are not healthy."

THE GREAT DISTINCTION

The distinction between exterior reality and interior reality we will label the great distinction. The great distinction is important because it is critical to understanding the nature of truth and because much of philosophical discourse since Descartes has to do with reality and our ability to perceive the way things are in reality. The great distinction is also critical in resolving the problem of universal concepts, about which there is debate among philosophers. Universal concepts are important because they have much to do with how words and terms are used, the use of language, so to speak.

Reality is everything that is (exists).

Everybody, at least subconsciously, accepts this. That is, if a thing exists, if it is real, it is a part of reality. The definition does not state what is real. It only states that if a thing exists in whatever form, it is a part of reality. Reality can be divided into objective (exterior) reality and subjective (interior) reality.

Objective reality is everything that exists outside the mind.

Subjective reality is everything that exists inside the mind.

This means a distinction always exists between the way things are in objective reality (outside the mind) and the way things are in subjective reality (inside the mind). Failure to make this distinction can lead to errors in philosophical positions.

So, the definition of reality includes things seen and unseen, outside the mind and all objects of thought inside the mind. For example the definition does not affirm the existence of God. It only affirms that if God exists, He is a part of reality. Likewise if ghosts exist they are a part of reality. If they do not exist they are not a part of reality. That is, they are not a part of objective reality. But they are certainly a part of subjective reality because the term god and ghosts stirs up images of these ephemeral beings in our mind. And if they do exist in the external world, they are a part of both objective and subjective reality, albeit in different forms.

From the extrapolation of this example, we can conclude that much of reality exists both outside the mind and as a perception inside the mind. That is, it exists both as objective reality and as a perception in subjective reality. Likewise there are things in objective reality of which the mind has no image or concept (a reasonable assumption). And there are things in subjective reality that do not exist in objective reality, such as each person's stream of consciousness or random thoughts, except those thoughts of images or ideas which represent things outside the mind.

When I think something like "I have a new idea for solving the energy crisis." That statement exists only in subjective reality. Now if I write that statement down on a piece of paper, like I just did, that statement now exists as symbols on paper in objective reality. It will also exist in subjective reality in the minds of everybody who reads it.

Plato held that ideas have existence outside the mind. That is, they exist in objective reality. We hold that they are the product of thought and as such they do not exist in objective reality except as symbols on paper, sound waves of speech or audio and video recordings. The impressions of these symbols and sound waves exist in the mind along with the universal concepts they represent.

We have painted a picture of reality according to basic philosophy. In the matter of rhetoric, however, it is a different story. People often find it useful to paint a different picture of reality to get a point across or to create an illusion.

There is much in literature about our ability to shape reality by our thinking. It is the way language is used and should be taken into consideration when participating in dialogue. Our thoughts do create subjective reality. And they create objective reality, but only to the extent that we act on them.

Technically speaking, if you make the great distinction (between exterior and interior reality), it becomes obvious that our thoughts do not create objective reality in the strict sense. A person's thoughts and belief system do, however, often determine the way a person perceives things (in objective reality). Here again is the classic confusion between truth and perception and the failure to make the distinction between interior and external reality.

There are, however, people who are not interested in technicalities or philosophy and this too needs to be taken into account in undertaking dialogue with one or more people. People are reluctant to let go of the illusions they maintain in their mind.

PHILOSOPHY HAS ITS PLACE

However philosophy has its place. In today's world there is so much confusion about what is right, what is wrong, what is true, what is false, what is real, what is not, one often gets the impression one can't be certain of anything.

There are some things of which we can be absolutely certain. These include the principles of mathematics, rules of logic, the most basic principles of reality and the laws of thought. These are the grounding rules of common sense, the foundation of all knowledge. They do not spring from religion or from science. They are elements of philosophy, gained from reason alone, common to every man. They provide a sense of security about life, knowing, knowledge and certitude, so that, if we know and understand them, we always have something to fall back on whenever we are faced with not knowing, confusion and doubt. They are like the rock of Gibraltar, unchanging, eternal, solid, time-tested and true.

Basic philosophy provides ultimate answers to our existence and the existence of the world around us. It tells us what reality is and our place in it. Philosophy affirms the validity of knowledge and our ability to know the way things are in reality. Philosophy tells us what truth is, teaches us to think correctly and gives us the tools to discern what is true and what is false.

Thomas Aquinas said philosophy is the handmaiden of theology. Actually, philosophy is the handmaiden of all disciplines since it provides the very foundation on which all knowledge rests and the rules of reason and research by which new discoveries are made.

Many in today's academic community, which is dominated by the analytic tradition as opposed to philosophy in the traditional, or generally accepted, sense, do not hold to this line of thought.[2]

Thou shalt not prevent anyone from speaking out.

CHAPTER IX
EXPLANATION OF RULES

All of these rules have ramifications and some are not as simple as they appear to be on the surface. Following is an explanation of each of these rules and why it is important that they be adhered to.

I. Everybody has the right to be heard, to make a statement and to change or retract it.

The flip side of this is the commandment to not prevent another person from speaking out or advancing a position. The reason is:

This right is guaranteed by the First Amendment to the Constitution of the United States of America. It says:

> Congress shall make no law respecting an establishment of religion or prohibiting the free exercise thereof, or abridging the freedom of speech, or of the press; or the right of the people peaceably to assemble, and to petition the Government for a redress of grievances.

This right is an integral element of democracy. It guarantees our freedom of expression. Therefore someone cannot deny a particular position or point of view from being disseminated as long as it has not been demonstrated to be false.

This means you have a right to believe what you want or decide to believe and to advance your position in public. Thus the first rule gives one the right to speak in public.

This right of freedom of speech has been upheld in many rulings by the U.S. Supreme Court, even the right to put your money where your mouth is, so to speak.

ACADEMIC FREEDOM

This right is also implied in the term, "academic freedom." The U.S. Supreme Court has identified academic freedom as a right protected by the First Amendment, which guarantees freedom of speech. Another affirmation of this right is the stand of the American Association of University Professors. According to the Statement of Principles of this association, "The common good depends on the free search for truth and its free exposition."

In summary then, the right to hold a position involves the right to be heard. And the right to be heard means you have the right to raise an issue. The right to change a position is inherent in our right to hold a position

II. Do not evade a question by addressing another issue or by responding to a question with a question.

The respondent must stick to the issue in question and not try to evade it.

Sidestepping an issue is a common tactic employed by members of Congress and political candidates who want to avoid addressing a particular question. Another tactic that is employed is responding to a question with another question, thus again evading the matter at issue. This is a trick to throw people off track.

This rule is repeatedly violated by politicians when asked questions by the media or in debates. A respondent to a question must address the issue posed by the question and not something unrelated to the question. All to often the questioner lets the respondent get away with not answering a question that is posed.

There is an exception to this rule, which on rare occasions needs to be made. Sometimes, in order to properly address the issue in question, it may be proper to clarify the question in order to answer it properly.

Even in public discourse there can be meaningful communication between the questioner and the respondent. Should public discourse reach this stage, there are a number of other elements that come into play. These are addressed at length in the Second Precept of Dialogue in the next-to-last chapter.

III. Do not make unsubstantiated claims, but verify what you say.

Any person making a categorical statement asserting one or more facts has the obligation to provide proof of the truth or validity of the facts asserted.

The political climate as of this writing was in great turmoil and many outrageous statements were being made. Rarely were any of them backed up with legitimate proof of their accuracy or their validity. The nature of proof is discussed in Chapter XII. This rule applies only to categorical statements asserting one or more facts. It does not apply to a person expressing an opinion.

This rule is probably violated by every lawmaker and every presidential candidate. We say "probably" because hopefully there are lawmakers and politicians who do not make unsubstantiated claims. We have not yet been able to identify them.

As noted in previous chapters, egregious violators of this rule were Mike Huckabee's assertion that Obama was raised in Kenya, the birther assertions of Donald Trump, and the numerous unsubstantiated claims by Michele Bachmann.

Some unsubstantiated examples are claims that Newt Gingrich's "baggage" makes him unfit to be president, Obama's policies have failed, government regulation is responsible for lack of job creation and economic growth.[1]

These are general statements implying that all (or at least most) policies of the Obama Administration have failed and that Obama has failed to lead. These statements might be true, but so far no evidence (that we are aware of) has been presented to prove that they are true. In addition they are negative universal statements which generally cannot be proven.

Negative particular statements are easier to prove. We have noted failed actions such as the Solyndra failure and "Fast and Furious."[2] But we have yet to identify policies and leadership that have failed, and a regulation that can be proven to be responsible for lack of job creation and economic growth. This does not mean they do not exist or cannot be identified. It only means we have not identified any and none have been called to our attention.

IV. Everybody has the obligation to not advance a statement or position that is false.

Nobody has the right to knowingly advance a falsehood.

This rule has been repeatedly violated by many in the media, by cable networks, by talking heads on some cable networks, by some presidential candidates and by some members of Congress.[3] Examples of these violation are listed in Chapters V and VI and include Donald Trump and Mike Huckabee.

This rule is violated by people who are simply mistaken and it is violated by people who advance a position as true all the while knowing it to be false. Often people who are mistaken will acknowledge their mistake. If they don't they fall in the same category as people who intentionally advance a false position.

People who intentionally advance a false position need to be called out and excoriated. Because of the fallout, a person who has been called out and excoriated in the media will likely think twice before acting in this manner again.

This is really a moral question and it puts the morality of the person who lies about a grievous matter in question. People simply do not have the right to deceive other people.

V. A person may not deliberately misrepresent another person's statement or point of view.

To deliberately misrepresent another person's point of view is dishonest.

This is another rule that has been repeatedly violated. The violation of it is particularly conspicuous in political advertising. The violation is also rife among members of Congress, some cable networks and some presidential candidates.[4] Misrepresentation of an opposing point of view is totally reprehensible. It amounts to a deliberate false statement.

There are many instances of the violation of this rule in the Republican presidential debates. It usually consists of taking statements out of context.

Romney made the statement that he would like to fire an insurance company. Jon Huntsman accused Romney of saying he liked issuing pink slips. This was a misquote of Romney's statement and a misrepresentation of his position.

Romney misrepresented Gingrich's position on legalizing illegal immigrants who have lived in their communities for 25 years and established relationships within the community. There are countless other examples which will be posted later.

VI. Any person has a right to disagree with the position(s) and/or statement(s) of any other person.

Opposition statements must be acknowledged.

Disagreement over an issue puts two people at odds with each other, which one or the other may be reluctant to acknowledge. This is a basic right and follows from the first Rule for Public Discourse. If a person has a right to his statement or position and it disagrees with another person's statement or position, then it follows that he has a right to disagree with that other person.

This rule needs to be stated since there may be occasions when proponents of a position will not acknowledge opposition statements. Whenever there is disagreement on a position or between two or more positions the proponent of a position needs to recognize the disagreement. If he fails to do so, he needs to be forced to acknowledge he is in violation of this rule. There can be no resolution to a disagreement when a proponent refuses to recognize the disagreement.

VII. All parties have the obligation to distinguish between a person and the position and/or statements of that person.

This is the classic ad hominem fallacy where the person is attacked rather than the argument of the person making it.

There is a very real tendency in people to attack a person holding a position they do not agree with. In fact this is a tactic often employed by politicians against their opponents. It is a fallacy of relevance.

The dictionary defines ad hominem as attacking a person's character to avoid discussing the issues. It occurs when instead of addressing the issue in question, a person attacks the character of the one making an assertion on the issue in question. The argument is fallacious because the character of a person is irrelevant to the position he is advancing or the argument he is making and has nothing to do with whether his argument is valid or not or his statement is true or correct or not.

Thus the assertion of a person must always be distinguished from the person making the assertion.

Romney was perhaps the most egregious violator of this rule in his attacks on Newt Gingrich, Jon Huntsman and others. He attacked Gingrich over his past. He attacked Huntsman for working for a Democratic president.

VIII. No one has the right to impute to another person beliefs, knowledge, understanding, ignorance, feelings, thoughts, intentions, positions or any other thing.

Nobody has the right to impute to another person any particular thing.

Imputing is a common mistake in public discourse. There was a lot of it going on in the Republican primary presidential debates. There is a tendency to accuse other people of lacking knowledge, understanding, intentions etc.

The fact is these kinds of judgments are likely to be wrong. It is not likely that one person can know what is in another person's mind. So this rule requires us to accept what another person says about his position or any other thing. If a person wants to know, then the thing to do is ask.

This precept echoes the Bible's admonition do not judge lest you be judged. Everybody has the right not only to his position, but to his beliefs, feelings, thoughts, intentions, likes and dislikes. These are integral to each person and only the person to whom they belong knows what they are.

Every person's ideas, beliefs, feelings, likes and dislikes differ in some degree from every other person's, ideas, beliefs, feelings, likes and dislikes.

Nobody has the right to tell another person what he (the other person) believes or what his feelings are or what his position is on any subject. Likewise another person's knowledge or ignorance is not a legitimate subject of speculation, except perhaps in an academic setting.

An example is Mitt Romney's often-made assertion that "the president does not understand how this economy works" and similar remarks. He is imputing what the president understands.

This rule is supported by the Third Rule, "Thou shalt not make unsubstantiated claims." A person who is imputing something to another person is not likely to be able to substantiate his claim, unless he is a mind reader.

IX. Negative universal statements are such that they generally cannot be proven and therefore cannot legitimately be made.

One should be on their guard for negative universal statements.

This rule is the subject of violations by individuals in all walks of life including in academia and in politics. You can't prove that you can't prove something. The reasoning behind this rule is not immediately obvious.

There is an objection that can be made to this rule because it is a negative universal statement. The objection is, "you can't prove a negative universal statement including this one."

This objection can be overcome by rewording it, viz., universal statements are such that they generally cannot be proven. This is a true statement and what it says is that each negative universal statement must be judged individually.

Conceivably exceptions exist. If and when they do exist, each individual exception would be immediately obvious. This is the case of negative particular statements. An example would be "there is no such thing as a square circle." The reason why there is no such thing as a square circle is discussed in Chapter XI.

Thus exceptions would be granted automatically if there were a case in which a negative universal could be proven. This would be rare and an example has failed recall by this author.

X. Fallacious or illogical arguments cannot legitimately be made or accepted.

Study of the fallacies and illogical arguments is a division of formal logic taught in most colleges and universities.

A common fallacy is the argument from ignorance. One example of the argument from ignorance was the conclusion of the Warren Commission that Lee Harvey Oswald was the lone gunman involved in the assassination of President John F. Kennedy because there was no evidence to determine otherwise. To use the argument that the fact that there was "no evidence" to determine otherwise is an argumentum ad ignorantiam.

The only logical conclusion one can draw from there being no evidence is that there is "no evidence" and one cannot logically draw any other conclusion. As it turned out the conclusion was not only logically incorrect, it was factually wrong as additional evidence was later discovered to determine otherwise.

CHAPTER X
WHAT IS TRUTH

We should all be in a quest for truth. This is the ultimate goal of philosophy. But what if one person has a different concept of truth than another person? Does this change one's perspective of what one is seeking? And can it change the way a statement is perceived by two or more people? If one is really seeking after truth, one needs to understand what truth is and what makes a thing or statement true.

Preliminary results of polls indicate that less than ten percent of adults can articulate a valid answer to what is truth. A substantial percentage of adults confuse truth with perception or actually have the wrong concept of what truth is. Many think truth is what the Bible says. Many think that truth depends on perception and is different for different people.[1]

With all these different perceptions going on, might we wonder about the nature of truth? If people don't have a common perception of what truth is, might we be in trouble trying to communicate? In other words might different perceptions of truth make a statement true for one person and false for another? How do we know that when we say, "This is true," and someone else says "This is false" about the same statement, that there is no such thing as truth? If this were the case about all statements, we would be in a sad state. It is like we are losing the meaning of the word, "truth." And this has even further implications, like we would be losing the meaning of a lot of words or terms. And this is not an all too far-fetched current state of affairs. In the writings of one of the founders of analytic philosophy, Ludwig Josef Johann Wittgenstein (1889-1951), he called it, "word games."

And so, how do we know that the person or persons we are talking to, doesn't have a different concept of what truth is than we do? The answer is, we don't. It is what Malcom Muggeridge (1903-1990) saw when he bemoaned the losing of the meaning of words.[2]

A COMMON UNDERSTANDING OF TRUTH

It doesn't have to be this way. We can do something about it. And we can start by establishing a common understanding of the nature of truth.

Polling indicates most Americans are confused about what truth is and what makes a thing or statement true. The fact they are unaware that they are confused does not alter the fact that they are not consciously aware of what constitutes truth. Subconsciously, or unconsciously, it is a different story.

Subconsciously, everybody, or nearly everybody, has the same notion about what truth is. If you want to know what a person really believes, you look at how the person acts or what the person says. We can tell what people really believe about truth by what they say. They say such things as, "That is not true... You are not telling the truth... I want the truth... That person lied, he did not tell the truth... That is true." In court a witness swears on the Bible that he will "tell the truth, the whole truth and nothing but the truth." The judge, the jury, the attorneys, the spectators, all know, or at least they think they know, what telling the truth amounts to.

In all these instances, everybody, or nearly everybody, has the same understanding of what truth is. That understanding consists of the accurate portrayal of events; the correct statement of facts, the correspondence in the mind of the way a thing is in reality. On the witness stand, telling the truth means to state where a defendant was at a given time. If he says he was somewhere else than where he really was is perjury.

TRUTH IS A CORRECT REPRESENTATION

Truth does not depend on one's perception. Truth is not what the Bible says or anyone else says. Truth is the correct representation of the way a thing is in reality.

Thus it does not depend on one's perception or what someone says. A thing is what it is and not something else and the truth about that thing reflects what it is in reality. Everybody, or nearly everybody, understands this, at least subconsciously.

Everybody talks about the truth, about what is true and not true. Yet hardly anybody can articulate what truth is. Outside of philosophers, hardly anybody bothers with consciously questioning what truth is. Knowing what truth is and what makes a thing true is important. Those who don't really understand what truth is are more at risk of being deceived than those who do understand what truth is.

One of the objects in serious discourse about philosophy, politics, business solutions, family matters is to reach agreement about the way a thing is in reality or about the best solution to a problem. This usually involves discovering the truth about something or discerning the truth or falsehood of a statement or representation.

RULES ARE ABOUT TRUTH

The rules for public discourse and precepts of dialogue are all about truth, or should be. In communicating our thoughts, desires, feelings, ideas, needs and other things we want to give the person or persons to whom we are talking or writing a true picture of what we want, of what we are thinking, of an idea we have or of how we are feeling. In describing a situation or a philosophical concept, we want to be able to convey an accurate description. That is to say, we want to get at the truth of the matter. To do this we must have a common understanding of what truth is.

While most professional philosophers will accept the correspondence theory of truth, the remaining plurality on technical grounds prefer different theories.

Basically, according to the correspondence theory, a thing or statement is true provided it corresponds to something, like a fact.

For our purposes here, we will liken the correspondence theory (which is relatively old) to the representational concept (which is relatively new). It is relatively new due to it being original to this book. So, according to both the representational concept and the correspondence theory, a thing is true if it corresponds to reality—to the way things are.

Ask 100 people to define truth and you will get many different answers. Strangely, it is rare that anyone will take the time to look up the definition in a dictionary. In informal polls of several hundred people, close to one-third of those interviewed voiced the opinion that truth was relative. That is that truth depended on each person's perception.

TRUTH IS NOT RELATIVE

Only a small minority were able to articulate a correct definition of truth. If truth were relative, there could be no moral standards. Lying, cheating, stealing, even killing, could be justified from the viewpoint of certain individuals. For the most part, people's unconscious understanding of what is truth is not relative. It is based in objective reality and the perception of that objective reality is the same for everybody. There is an objective standard that everybody unconsciously accepts.

People who make the truth dependent on their viewpoint, that is relative to them, are not being honest with themselves. They are making truth the way they want it to be and thereby divorcing it from objective reality. If a person is seriously out of touch with objective reality, he is said to be neurotic. Granted, there is an element of inexactness in the way we perceive external reality. But inexactness is different from relative.

A woman who held a master's degree in education from Harvard University said in answer to the poll in 2007, "Truth has always perplexed me. When I discuss this with people, they always have their own version. I am honestly unclear about what truth is."

Many great philosophers have expounded on what truth is and what makes a thing or statement true. Among them is Saikat Guha. For those philosophically inclined, the following is his technical analysis of what constitutes truth.[4]

[The "truth-maker principle"] enjoys wide-spread acceptance among contemporary philosophers and seems fairly self-evident... It says that what is true is determined by what there is. In other words, truth supervenes on reality; what exists determines what the world is like, or which truths obtain.

This is sometimes put by saying that every truth must have a truth-maker, something which, by existing, makes that truth obtain or be the case. A truth may have several truth-makers, which jointly support that truth (by all existing together), but it must have at least one. A more precise formulation of this principle may be made by reflecting that, for each existing thing, there is the truth, about that thing, that it exists. Thus, assuming that I exist, there is a truth about me which states my existence, and there is another for you, another for Lyndon Johnson, and so on. Let us call these particular existential truths. (We should understand these as the sort of truths that are expressed by singular existential sentences featuring proper names, like "Socrates exists". Of course we do not need to have proper names for all objects, or to know that they exist, in order for the relevant truths to obtain—they just have to exist.) Then there is a further truth which says, of all things taken together, that these are all the things that exist (that is, there are no other things besides these). This truth, together with the particular existential truths, are what we may call the basic existential truths. Then the truth-maker principle states that the basic existential truths jointly entail all truths. In other words, each and every truth supervenes on the basic existential truths, taken together. This formulation avoids a problem of the earlier version: we need not be puzzled about what makes anti-existential claims, like "There are no unicorns", true. There need not be any separate truth-makers for such a claim; rather it is entailed by the basic existential truths jointly, since there is nothing in the list that is a unicorn, and it says at the end of the list that there is nothing else.

CHAPTER XI
THE USE OF LANGUAGE

Much of philosophy of the last century was concerned with the analysis of language. Much of this study of language was concerned with the use of words and to an extent with the relation of words with concepts. There was debate over the existence of "universals." There were some who doubted the relevance of universal concepts and to some extent the nature of the distinction between external reality (everything outside the mind) and internal reality (everything inside the mind), though it may not have been couched in those terms. Without this distinction, definitions are devalued and class distinctions are blurred.

There are people who are at fault in communicating because they use terms with which other people are unfamiliar. A rich vocabulary is to be admired. Even in simple everyday discourse we use terms that other people do not understand and other people use terms we do not understand. It makes us appear erudite. This probably occurs more often then we think. There is even a common expression for it. We, or they, are said to be "talking over their, or our, heads." The root cause of misunderstanding is often lack of people having the same, or even any, understanding of the meaning of certain terms being used. We just don't know the extent of another person's vocabulary.

There are different tacks we can take from here. We can take up the whole theory of language as developed by a whole string of philosophers. This clearly is beyond the scope of this book, let alone this chapter. Or we can simplify matters by dealing with how written and spoken words communicate meaning from one person to one or more other persons. That is we can look into how words create data in the mind.

Meaningful communication involves sending and receiving information in the form of verbal or written words. For words to be meaningful they must represent something in the mind such as images, ideas and concepts. These images, ideas and concepts are communicated by means of terms. Terms consist of one or more words. For terms to have meaning they must represent precisely the same thing to the person using them as to the person or persons receiving them. That is, they must represent the same concept to each person involved in dialogue or any other form of discourse. Therefore, they must be explained or defined so that every person has the same understanding of what is meant.

USE OF DEFINITIONS

Most terms used in every day speech have a generally accepted meaning to the people using them. But often, even in every day speech, one or more terms will be misunderstood by one or more people communicating with each other. In philosophical dialogue and in technical and legal matters this is a problem. To avoid this, definitions are employed.

The terms we use exist both in external reality and internal reality. In external reality these terms consist of words or symbols on paper or sounds if we speak them. These words written or spoken also exist as an exact copy in internal reality—the mind.

Terms in the mind exist in two forms, an image of how they appear in external reality and either an image or concept for what they represent. Thus we can define image as a concrete representation of an object in external reality such as that individual person named Harry or that certain Ford car with a dent in the fender. The image evoked in the mind is a picture of the Ford and the picture of the term.

DEFINITION OF CONCEPT IS IMPORTANT

We can define concept as an abstract piece of data that per se exists only in internal reality. Thus we can abstract from the image of that particular Ford and form a concept of carness: encompassing all cars; or Ford car: all cars made by Ford Motor Company, and apply these two concepts to each individual car or each individual car made by Ford Motor Company. But in another sense a concept may also exist in external reality in the form of a term by which we communicate what we mean when we write or speak the word car or Ford (car). This term, in turn, is represented in the mind as a concrete image by which the abstract concept is given meaning.

Now here is where it gets a little complicated and philosophers have gone off in all different directions to explain how it works.

We will keep it simple and obvious. There are two parts of an abstract concept as it exists in the mind. The abstract part of it does not per se exist in external reality, but the term we use to describe the abstract part exists in both internal reality and external reality in the form of the term we use to communicate it.

We can understand how the term "courage" or "beauty" exists outside the mind but not the concept itself, which we can apply to different aspects of it in external reality. Technically speaking, we can only form a new concept through descriptions or definitions of it. We can also learn a new concept by experience over time, such as by how other people use the term of "courage" or "beauty."

WORDS THAT ARE NOT A TERM

For proof or justification of this explanation, we can conjure up illogical "terms" that are only words and don't exist in the mind except as words. Take the words "square circle." We can say or write the words "square circle." But "square circle" is not a term because we cannot conceive of how a "square circle" looks and we cannot draw a "square circle." It is just two words spoken or written, that really have no representation in external reality except as symbols on paper or sounds of speech.

Great thinkers do not necessarily need words or terms to create great thoughts. They only need words or terms in communicating those great thoughts to others in the outside world. Thus we are in conflict with those who reduce philosophy to language in that we are reducing language to a secondary role of communicating thoughts—the ideas and concepts—that great thinkers, or anyone else, has produced. In our position, language—words and terms—are secondary while ideas and concepts are primary.

SUBJECTIVE REALITY

All images, concepts, ideas—all thoughts—are a part of subjective reality. They may not exist in the real word or in objective reality. In a practical sense, only an image in the mind exists as its object outside the mind. In an abstract sense, symbols on paper or other media, may represent in the external world abstract concepts that exist in the mind.

IMAGES DIFFER FROM CONCEPTS

In other words, particular things which images represent exist in objective reality as do things that can't be seen or touched or that have no mass which are represented by concepts. Examples of things in objective reality that are represented by concepts are electricity, atoms and sub-atomic particles. They are represented by concepts because we do not have images of them. We only have images of the words written or spoken by which we communicate concepts. And it is a reasonable assumption that only a tiny part of objective or external reality is perceived by men and thus is represented in the collective mind of man.

It is important to note that the same image or concept may be conjured up in different ways with different words making up different terms. Thus two philosophers or politicians or lawmakers might be in disagreement about a position because of the terms they use and/or the description they employ.

In effect they might hold the same position, but use different terms to describe it. The disagreement may be resolved by distinguishing and defining descriptions and terms. Preliminary analysis of responses by philosophers in polling on the concept of truth indicate this is the case to at least some degree involving the various theories being proffered.

The problem of universals, in which there is currently debate, is another instance in which different terms may be used to apply to the same concepts.

CHAPTER XII
THE NATURE OF PROOF

The purpose of proof is to determine what to believe and what not to believe. Understanding how the nature of proof fits into the scheme of things will aid in the determination of what to believe and what not to believe and in recognizing unsubstantiated claims.

There are probably few students majoring in philosophy who have not heard a professor say "You cannot prove" this or that. One of the more common statements is "You cannot prove the existence of external reality," or something to that effect. What is left unsaid is: "You cannot prove that you cannot prove the existence of external reality."

Generally speaking, as proffered in previous chapters, a negative universal cannot be proven. It can be disproved, but not proven. Many, probably most, negative particular propositions cannot be proven. They can be disproved by proving the existence of facts that contradict the negative proposition.

It should be noted that the Ninth Rule for Public Discourse states *Negative universal statements are such that they generally cannot be proven and therefore cannot legitimately be made.* In nearly all cases in which a negative universal statement is made, it is immediately obvious that it cannot be proven

WHAT IS PROOF

Just what is proof and of what does it consist? It is likely we have all been confronted at one time or another with the challenge of "prove it!" How do we prove something and more importantly to whom do we "prove it!"

There are many ramifications to these questions, which are not immediately obvious. One of these ramifications is that statements, which claim that this or that proves this or that, may be false in that they prove no such thing. As we have seen statements that this or that proves a negative proposition is very likely to be a false claim.

However, there are proofs that are valid and do prove what they purport to prove. For example, statements that this or that proves a proposition are based either on conclusions drawn from a priori premises (deductive reasoning) or empirical evidence. In all cases of a priori reasoning, conclusions are true if the premises are true and the argument is valid. Whether the premises are true is often determined by empirical evidence. Empirical evidence rests either on scientific facts or, as in law, on the rules of evidence. The validity of an argument is determined by the rules of logic.

For a person to be justified in his belief of a particular thing, he must have proved to himself that it is true. Our definition of proof (which is practical) is: *Anything at all that conclusively demonstrates that a thing is the way it is represented to be.* This is the concept of proof in the real world of common sense.

FLAT EARTH SOCIETY

Here is an example of a thing that has been conclusively demonstrated to be true. There were people at certain periods of history who believed the earth to be flat. Science has demonstrated conclusively that the earth is round. The evidence is so conclusive that we all accept that (except members of the Flat Earth Society).

Which brings up the question of majority agreement involving particular positions. This used to be expressed as "counting cabbages" (heads), which does not determine whether a statement is true or false. However, the fact that there is disagreement on whether a particular statement is true or false, is not a determining factor either. In the academic climate of today there are very few positions in which there will not be one or more individuals holding an opposing viewpoint, especially on matters of philosophy. And where there is a consensus on a particular theory or position held by a majority of professionals in a particular discipline, it may be a good indication (not proof) that that particular position is true, particularly if there is only a minor fringe element such as the flat earth society in opposition.

Such is the case when we state there is conclusive proof the earth is round, it rotates on its axis and it revolves around the sun. We are totally justified in believing this based on empirical evidence.

We are also justified in believing the principles of mathematics, physics and other sciences and the basic principles of reality such as the principle of contradiction formulated by Aristotle in his Metaphysics.

THE "TO WHOM" FACTOR

There are those who will say these cannot be proved (a negative universal), which brings up the subject of "to whom" this or that can or cannot be proved. The "to whom" factor is at the heart of what the nature of proof consists. The "to whom" factor has three applications. They are individual, communal and theoretical. The first two have to do with the practical world of common sense. The third has to do with the esoteric world of theories. The first application is individual. It is up to each individual to decide what to believe or not to believe, what to accept into his belief system or exclude from his belief system.

As stated before, a belief system is the totality of beliefs of a philosophy, a religion or an individual. In regard to the individual it is the sum total of what he consciously believes to be true. In this sense proof that a thing is true or false consists in what each individual is justified in believing. Each individual must justify (prove) to himself that such and such is true.

The second application involves demonstrating to one or more other people that a thing is the way it is represented to be. Thus this application of proof revolves around persuasion, because we cannot force another person or group of people to accept our proof of something.

Fortunately, in philosophical discourse, there are rules for doing this, which makes one's position and/or arguments or "proof" subject to objective review. Traditionally, these include the principles and rules of logic and metaphysics. It is through observance of these principles and rules that we can justify to ourselves and others that our premises are true and that our arguments are valid.

INVICNIBLE IGNORANCE

There are those who, no matter how convincing the evidence, will not accept a thing to be true or false. People in this category are termed logically invincible. A person who rigidly maintains a position despite conclusive evidence to the contrary commits the fallacy of invincible ignorance. A person who is logically invincible is not a good subject with whom to engage in meaningful communication.

The third application of "to whom" is more often to nobody and to everybody and consists of professional theorizers (generally university professors or scientists) making the case of why a certain position or theory is correct or incorrect, or best explains something. This third option is characterized by some philosophers as proving something to the universe.

Thus in light of this review of the nature of proof, many statements that purport to prove something or make a case for something do no such thing. It is an old philosophical adage that when approaching certain subjects, that we maintain a "healthy skepticism." When we do, we are more likely to spot statements that falsely purport to prove something. This is particularly true in regard to negative statements. All this is relevant to the rules for public discourse in which we hold public officials accountable and constructive dialogue in which two or more people pursue resolutions to disputed questions.

CHAPTER XIII
BELIEF SYSTEMS

A brief word about belief systems is relevant here. Everybody has a conscious belief system and at least one subconscious belief system. A belief system is the sum total of all beliefs held by a person or within the parameters of a particular theory, position or entity such as an explanation of a phenomenon, a philosophy, a religion or a sect. It is likely that most, if not all, personal, philosophical and religious belief systems contain certain beliefs that are false.

There are lawmakers who hold positions (beliefs) that are contradictory to the positions of other lawmakers. From this, using the principle of contradiction, we can conclude that there are beliefs (viewpoints) of lawmakers that are false. Take two viewpoints that contradict each other. One is necessarily false. This does not mean that one position or viewpoint is true, since both may be false.

In constructive dialogue, the belief systems of the people involved may need to be taken into account because certain beliefs tend to be an obstacle to resolving conflict and reaching solutions to problems. In many, instances, beliefs that are obstacles to dialogue are based on false information, false philosophy, or just a plain bad attitude such as a dislike of another person or of another person's position.

In order for Congress to reach solutions to the problems facing it, there must be created a willingness of its members to engage in meaningful communication with each other. Lawmakers who refuse to do this can be easily identified.

They will be the ones who consistently violate the Rules for Public Discourse.

For Congress to function efficiently, members must engage in constructive dialogue. To engage in constructive dialogue, they must observe precepts of dialogue. It would also help if they observed rules of civility. Rules of Civility are listed in Chapter XV and Precepts of Dialogue are listed and explained in Chapter XVI.

Meaningful communication is a special kind of discourse in which the Precepts of Dialogue are observed. For meaningful communication to take place, there needs to be an element of trust generated between the participants. Many people are neurotic in this regard, perhaps because they are protecting beliefs in their belief system they unconsciously know are false.

TWO BELIEF SYSTEMS

Psychologists tell us we have two belief systems, one conscious and one subconscious. We often don't know what our subconscious beliefs are until we act on them or are unable to act because of them. They at times may result in anti-social behavior.

The ultimate purpose of meaningful communication is to arrive at the truth of any given matter and thereby enhance our understanding of the way things are. This may involve reaching agreements and solving problems. The basic premise is that the truth cannot harm your belief system or you.

In reviewing various issues with people, some have become angry at being asked their opinion on the definition of truth and at the Precepts of Dialogue. They have a fear of being hemmed in. Confronted with it a prominent attorney said, "I hate to be set up to be proven wrong and stupid." Another person, a counselor, said, "I don't believe in definitions and I don't need rules to communicate."

These people were adamant and refused to even engage in constructive dialogue. It was impossible to talk to them about certain ideas and concepts. A number of people in various professions have responded the same way.

There are people who do not believe two plus two always equals four. There are people who do not accept one or more basic principles. And there are people, as previously stated, who will not accept an established fact no matter how convincing the proof.

It is not within the scope of this book to deal with the psychological aspects of belief systems, which determine who we are and how we act. What is relevant to this discussion is how we can determine which of our beliefs are true and which are false.

Using established philosophical principles, these rules and certain investigative procedures we (and anyone else, for that matter) can make determinations of what is true and what is false about many things, and what to believe and what not to believe about all things.

CHAPTER XIV
THE PRESS AND THE MEDIA

There was generally balanced reporting of the political scene in Washington by most newspapers, the three major networks, ABC, NBC and CBS, and Cable Channel CNN. Generally acknowledged as conservative minded was the Fox News Channel with a bias against Democrats. Generally acknowledged as liberal minded was MSNBC with a bias against Republicans.

It all blew up the night of the presidential debate two days before the South Carolina primary January 21, 2012 and Republicans and Fox News had a field day airing their grievances against the "biased liberal media." Prominent among the objects of the name-calling were the New York Times, CNN, ABC News, NBC News, CBS News and members of the Press in general. .

Republicans have long accused journalists and the "liberal media" of bias against them. The Washington press corps and most journalists are generally fair-minded and try to be balanced in their reporting. It is easy for bias to creep in to the selection of stories and the questions asked. Journalists generally abide by the Rules for Public Discourse in that they check their facts and don't misrepresent what they report on.

There are, however, some reporters who cross the line in the facts they report (and sometimes misrepresent), the way they report the news, in the people they interview and the way they insert themselves into a story.

At any rate, the exchange between John King and Newt Gingrich again brought into the open the smoldering resentment among Republicans of many in the media.

King of CNN was moderator of the Thursday night debate and started out by asking Gingrich to comment on his ex-wife's assertion made in an interview with ABC News and the Washington Post that he asked her for an "open marriage." Gingrich objected to this and went off on a blistering attack of King, CNN, ABC News, the "liberal media" and the press in general.

NO VIOLATION OF RULES

Neither King nor Gingrich violated the Rules for Public Discourse in the way they handled themselves. King really had no choice but to pose the question. Gingrich responded to the accusation, which he said was false. He also exercised his right given him in the First Rule to advance an issue.

It was argued among the various pundits and the case may be made that ABC News crossed the line in airing unsubstantiated accusations just before the debate and just before the South Carolina primary election.

A free press is what makes a democracy possible. And a restricted press is what makes an autocratic regime possible. This imposes a certain responsibility on members of a free press and a free media. The two are not the same.

Journalism was in prior decades a more separate discipline in colleges and universities than it is now. Thus there were bachelors, masters and doctoral degrees in journalism. Journalism is more and more becoming a division of communication. Thus the degrees conferred may more likely be a bachelor of arts in communication with a journalism emphasis. This is further divided into print journalism and broadcast journalism, which is further divided into radio and television. A whole new division that has emerged is information technology (IT) dealing with the Internet.

ONLY WAY NEWS DISTRIBUTED

Up through the first few decades of the last century, the print media—newspapers and magazines—were practically the only way the news was distributed. Starting in the third and fourth decades—the 1920s and 1930s—radio took over a portion of the way the news was distributed.

Starting after World War II, television entered the picture and by mid century was a third way the news was distributed. Starting in the last decade of the last century, more and more people were connected to the Internet until today it has become a fourth major way in which the news is distributed.

Up into much of the second half of the last century, journalists were held to and generally maintained high standards in the way the news was reported. There was not as much of the bias and the outright slanting of news that is prevalent in some of the media today.

OWNERSHIP CONCENTRATED

In much of the last century, many independent radio and television stations sprang up, competing with each other in major markets. Beginning in the last two or three decades of the last century, major networks began buying up and consolidating smaller newspapers, radio and television stations so that ownership is more and more concentrated in a few media conglomerates. This has led to a greater temptation to manage the news by some cable networks such as Fox News and certain networks of radio stations.

To complicate matters further, are the bloggers and postings to social media in which there is still less constraint to be accurate and impartial.

This then is the scene in which the 112th Congress and the 2012 election year played out. Much of the information we are daily confronted with is false. It is more and more important for people to be made aware of the nature of truth and what makes a statement true.

It is further more and more important that people be made aware of the many ways that false information can be couched in believable scenarios and the public deceived or misled. Elections have been and can be won and lost on false statements made for public consumption. There is a tendency of people to come to believe a statement is true based on its constant repetition.

DECEPTION NEEDS TO BE IDENTIFIED

This kind of public deception needs to be identified and excoriated. People now have the means of making public (publicizing) false statements, misrepresentations and fallacious arguments and those who make them. But to be most effective, identifying false statements needs to be a function of the press. There are many members of the fourth estate who maintain a high standard of morality and integrity. And there are instances in today's media frenzy of reporters pointing out false statements and misrepresentations by political candidates and members of congress.

There is one instance that stood out during the writing of this chapter. The campaign of Mitt Romney aired a television advertisement quoting President Obama as saying in the 2008 presidential campaign, "If we keep talking about the economy, we are going to loose." This was a partial quote of Obama. This is the actual statement that Obama made: "Senator McCain's campaign actually said, and I quote, 'If we keep talking about the economy, we are going to loose.'"

The ad conveniently left out "Senator McCain's campaign actually said, and I quote." It was reported that Romney stood by the ad. CNN newsman John King spent a whole segment of air time exposing this deception. This is an example of what the press can do and is doing in holding candidates accountable.

Another example of misrepresentation by Romney was the failure to recognize a key element of Newt Gingrich's position on immigration. Gingrich said he was opposed to amnesty. He proposed a third alternative to the dilemma of allowing illegal immigrants, who have lived here for 25 years, raised a family, paid taxes and been productive citizens, a way out in order to avoid deportation. This third alternative would grant them a special legal status that would not allow them a path to citizenship.

VIOLATION OF FIFTH RULE

Romney characterized Gingrich's position as amnesty and refused to accept the distinction.[1] It was assumed that granting illegal immigrants amnesty, would allow them to later become U.S. citizens. This is another instance of Romney's misrepresentation of a position.

In Romney's defense, the two positions on immigration are similar. But there is a technical difference. Had Romney made the distinction between Gingrich's position that ruled out future citizenship and amnesty, his argument against Gringrich's position would still have pretty much the same force, and would not have been a misrepresentation. Romney did not have to employ a dishonest characterization to make his point.

It is the role of the press to investigate unsubstantiated claims and false statements and to alert the public of statements that are false and/or are unsubstantiated. It doesn't hurt to remind reporters of their obligation in this regard. It won't hurt to alert them that there are now Rules for Public Discourse by which they can hold lawmakers, candidates and everyone else accountable for what they say.

CHAPTER XV
OTHER RULES

There are other rules that would help to make Congress more productive. These are Rules of Civility and Precepts of dialogue, which, if followed, would help in reaching agreements, finding solutions and resolving conflicts.[1]

Rules of civility apply to good manners and etiquette. Rules for Public Discourse apply to public statements by lawmakers and others. Precepts of Dialogue are rules which apply to constructive discourse between two or more people about a specific subject and may or may not be public.

In some cases, such as public hearings in Congress, objectives of Rules for Public Discourse and Precepts of Dialogue overlap. Participants need to be held accountable and determinations need to be made. Likewise, some of the Rules and Precepts are similar or the same, but oriented differently toward their different objectives. And, of course, rules of civility are supplements to both objectives.

There were rules of civility which were generally accepted and observed by nearly everybody in this country up through the first half of the last century. They were exemplified by good manners which were codified in all areas of human endeavor by Emily Post in her voluminous tome, *Emily Post's Etiquette: The Blue Book of Social Usage*.[2]

Hopefully, by the end of the next chapter, the reasons for each set of rules and an understanding of each rule, and how it can be used will obtain. There are many more rules of civility than the ones listed below. The ones listed below are chosen because they apply to communication.

Observance of the rules of civility marked a person of "breeding," a person of good upbringing who had (at that time) a sense of propriety and "style" or "class." It was taken for granted that these rules were always (and perhaps still are) observed by "gentlemen," the nobility and members of the "upper class," which in America usually signified "old money" and the Eastern establishment.

CIVILITY AND PROPRIETY

Civility and the collective sense of propriety effectively reined in outlandish behavior up through the first half of the last Century. Civility and propriety progressively diminished in the latter decades of the Century. People with agendas are now going to greater lengths to press their cause, gain legislation and persuade other people to their way of thinking. Many are in violation of the rules propounded in this book.

Rules of civility are not a necessary ingredient to discerning integrity in public discourse. But they are relevant to alerting one to the lack of a sense of propriety by the person violating them, possibly the lack of good judgment and certainly the lack of good taste.

As a young man, George Washington made up a list of 110 rules of civility. There are a number of books that list them. They are variously entitled *George Washington'sRules of Civility, George Washington's Rules of Civility and Decent Behavior in Company and Conversation* and similar titles.[3]

Following is a sampling of George Washington's Rules of Civility that apply to communication:

1. Every action done in company ought to be with some sign of respect to those that are present.

12. Shake not the head, feet, or legs; roll not the eyes; lift not one eyebrow higher than the other, wry not the mouth, and bedew no man's face with your spittle by approaching too near him when you speak.

19. Let your countenance be pleasant but in serious matters somewhat grave.

47. Mock not nor jest at any thing of importance. Break no jests that are sharp, biting, and if you deliver any thing witty and pleasant, abstain from laughing thereat yourself.

49. Use no reproachful language against any one; neither curse nor revile.

58. Let your conversation be without malice or envy, for 'tis a sign of a tractable and commendable nature, and in all causes of passion permit reason to govern.

64. Break not a jest where none take pleasure in mirth; laugh not aloud, nor at all without occasion; deride no man's misfortune though there seem to be some cause.

65. Speak not injurious words neither in jest nor earnest; scoff at none although they give occasion.

66. Be not forward but friendly and courteous, the first to salute, hear and answer; and be not pensive when it's a time to converse.

73. Think before you speak, pronounce not imperfectly, nor bring out your words too hastily, but orderly and distinctly.

74. When another speaks, be attentive yourself and disturb not the audience. If any hesitate in his words, help him not nor prompt him without desired. Interrupt him not, nor answer him till his speech be ended.

89. Speak not evil of the absent, for it is unjust.

We will not belabor all the rules of civility listed in various treatises, many of which are not relevant to the current discussion. We have composed the following rules of civility, which are relevant to behavior in public and private discourse in today's world.

1. Be kind and considerate.
> *Rudeness is not helpful to communicating or understanding.*

2. Do not criticize or attack another person.
> *It is never necessary to attack another person. Attack the other person's argument not his person.*

3. Do not interrupt in the middle of another person's discourse.
> *This is just bad manners and detracts from the person interrupting.*

4. Do not become angry or express anger.
Expressing anger is counter productive to any endeavor

5. Be tactful in expressing disagreement with another person's point of view.
This is an important element of being considerate.

6. Do not make inappropriate jokes or other remarks.
This is another important element in being considerate.

8. Be attentive. Do not act bored. Be a good listener.
This is another element in being considerate.

9. Be respectful. Do not disparage any person in any way.
This is another element of good manners.

10. Do not engage in inappropriate laughter.
It is bad manners.

11. Do not mumble. Speak distinctly and enunciate carefully.
It will help in communicating what you have to say.

12. Search for basic agreements.
It helps in establishing rapport.

13. Search for strength in other positions.
This also helps in establishing rapport.

14. Do not use loud and boisterous language.
It is not polite.

15. Watch how you say things.
Often how you say things confers more meaning than what you say.

CHAPTER XVI
PRECEPTS OF DIALOGUE

The Precepts of Dialogue are about meaningful communication in which two or more people reach a higher level of understanding. There is much written on dialogue and there are even organizations that promote it.[1]

As previously stated, Precepts of Dialogue are rules which apply to constructive discourse between two or more people about a specific subject. Rules for Public Discourse are about statements made by people usually in the public eye for public consumption. Precepts of Dialogue, on the other hand, apply to discussion of issues in more personal settings such as a position in philosophy, or an issue before a city council or other political subdivisions, or a public hearing in Congress about a specific matter. The dialogue may be a private discussion or it may be open to the public.

In some cases, such as public hearings in Congress, objectives of Rules for Public Discourse and Precepts of Dialogue overlap. Participants need to be held accountable and determinations need to be made. Likewise, some of the rules and precepts are similar or the same, but oriented differently toward their different objectives. And, of course, the rules of civility are supplements to both.

Communication between two or more people is such an important factor in the quality of our lives that we all need to work on it. Few would argue there is no room for improvement in their lives. And communication is a major factor. Communication takes effort. It's work. Here, in this chapter, are some constructive steps to make it work and which can be applied to judge the abilities of those holding public hearings or doing panel discussions.

The following Precepts of Dialogue are especially powerful tools that can be used to enhance communication in general and dialogue in particular. What makes them powerful is how they can be used. This is discussed in the next chapter.

There are major implications to each of these Precepts that are not immediately obvious. The first nine Precepts of Dialogue and the first nine Rules for Public Discourse are similar to each other and compliment each other as does the Tenth Rule and the Thirteenth Precept. Since the objectives of the Rules and the Precepts are different, they are stated differently.

There are an additional three Precepts that are not of practical use in the Rules for Public Discourse and therefore are not listed under them. These are Precepts X, XI and XII. Similarities and differences of the first nine Rules and Precepts and the Tenth Rule and Thirteenth Precept are recognized in the explanation of the Precepts..

We will first list all the precepts and afterwards explain the implications of each precept.

REVIEW OF PRECEPTS

I. Everybody has a right to his position, to state it, define it and change it, and the right to make a statement and to change or retract it.

II. In dialogue, the respondents have the obligation to address the issued being advanced.

III. Any person advancing a position and/or making one or more statements has the obligation to explain them and provide proof of their truth or validity.

IV. No one has the right to advance a false statement or position.

V. In dialogue the respondents have the obligation to correctly understand and accept the statement(s) and/or position(s) being advanced.

VI. Any person has a right to disagree with the position of any other person.

VII. All parties have the obligation to distinguish between a person and the position of that person.

VIII.. All parties have the obligation to not impute to another person beliefs, knowledge, understanding, ignorance, feelings, thoughts, intentions, positions or any other thing.

IX. A negative universal statement may not be used in an argument or to make a point.

+X. The person making a statement or maintaining a position has a right to verify that all his statements and his positions are correctly understood.

+XI. Any person maintaining a position has the right and obligation to distinguish and define (within the rules of logic) the terms and concepts he uses.

+XII. All those involved in constructive dialogue have the obligation to accept and use the terms and concepts as defined by the person advancing a position.

XIII. All parties have the obligation to observe the rules of logic and identification of fallacies.

These Rules are the tenets of responsible discourse. Everybody, or nearly everybody, will accept and use them when they are apprised of their existence. For those individuals who will not accept one or more of these Rules and Precepts, then this is the first issue to be resolved, hopefully by the process outlined herein, namely, constructive dialogue. Following is an explanation.

I. Everybody has a right to his position, to state it, define it and change it, and the right to make a statement and to change or retract it.

> This precept corresponds with the First Rule for Public Discourse, *Thou shalt not prevent anyone from speaking out.*
>
> That everyone has a right to believe what he wants or decides to believe is a fundamental right recognized by law in Democratic countries and by society. It is an adjunct of freedom of speech. It is also inherent in the moral responsibility that each person must take for his actions. If each person is responsible for his actions then he must have

the right to govern those actions since his actions are governed by what he chooses to believe in.

A position is a particular belief, point of view or stand a person holds to. A particular belief or position can usually be summed up in a brief statement. And as such can be analyzed and debated. Thus a particular position can become an issue in meaningful communication. And each person has a right to his position and to change it.

We acknowledge that a person has a right to his position and the right to advance his position in public. We also acknowledge that a person does not have the right to deceive other people in ways that will harm other people or society.

And now we come to an additional right. And that is the right to change one's position, at will. We are all in a search for truth or should be. If we can be shown that a position we hold is false, we must change it. For many, depending on the position we or they are about to change, this moment can be a catharsis. It is something that could change our lives.

The right to change our position is inherent in our right to hold a position. Implied in this right is the obligation that a person committed to meaningful communication must be willing to change his position if he can be shown that it is false. We are not dealing with courtroom drama here. What we are talking about is a friendly exchange of ideas that can lead an individual to a new understanding of the truth of the way a thing is in reality.

In summary then, the right to hold a position involves the right to be heard. And the right to be heard means you have the right to raise an issue. The right to change your position is inherent in your right to hold a position

II. In dialogue, the respondents have the obligation to address the issue being advanced and not something else.

This precept corresponds with the Second Rule for Public Discourse: *Thou shalt not evade a question by addressing another issue or responding to a question with a question.*

Responding to a question by addressing a whole separate issue was seen in the presidential debates and in interviews with the candidates and others. The Second Rule for Public Discourse aptly disallows this. While responding to this evasion is applicable to public discourse, in dialogue between two or more people it is less an issue since it is easily discerned and disallowed.

There is another aspect of this precept that applies more to dialogue and that is arguing beside the point. It is thus launching into a lengthy argument that purports to prove one thing, but actually proves something else.

For example, a lawmaker seeking to justify the Administration's mandate that requires everybody to purchase health insurance argues that universal health care is owed to every citizen. That really has nothing to do with the mandate.

The reason for the mandate is to lower the cost of insurance by providing a pool of people with less health care needs to offset the cost of people with health care needs that occasion more claims.

This is called the fallacy of ignoratio elenchi. It is also named by other logicians the fallacy of irrelevant conclusions or irrelevant theses.

III. Any person advancing a position and/or making one or more statements has the obligation to provide proof of their truth or validity.

This Precept corresponds to the Third Rule of Public Discourse: *Thou shalt not make unsubstantiated claims*

This precept imposes an additional obligation on the communicator in addition to providing proof that his position or statement is true.

The additional obligation puts the burden of being understood on the communicator. Often when a person is not understood it is because he is not adequately presenting his position.

Generally speaking, whenever there is a right there is a corresponding obligation. The First Precept establishes the right to hold a position.

The Second Precept imposes the obligation on the respondents to address the issue being advanced. The Third Precept imposes the obligation on the communicator to make himself understood.

The Third Precept imposes the obligation on the communicator to explain or elaborate on what his position consists, give reasons why it is valid, provide proof or evidence that what he says is correct or true and submit to questioning.

Where communication often breaks down, whether in informal talk or in meaningful communication, is when the one advancing a position does not make clear exactly what his position is. Sometimes a position is not clear to the one advancing it. It behooves the one advancing a position and the one or ones receiving it to question the other regarding his or their perception of it.

With certain exceptions, it is the fault of the communicator if his position is not understood. There will be instances when other people will not want to understand another's position whether from lack of patience or just a plain closed mindedness or even prejudice against a person advancing a position.

In these instances, this is not the fault of the communicator. In these instances, there may not be much he can do. But if he has a willing audience, it is up to him to make himself understood.

There will be people who are communicating a position who will not accept this. They will be people who think their audience is not capable of understanding their esoteric positions. Or they will be people who think other people are not worthy of their pearls of wisdom. This attitude is a violation of this precept. In nearly all instances of a lack of understanding of another's position, it is because the person explaining it is not doing a good enough job in expressing himself. It is unlikely that one will find a person willing to engage in meaningful communication, who does not have the ability to understand any position or theory when it is properly explained.

IV. No one has the right to advance a false position.

This precept corresponds to the Fourth Rule for Public Discourse: *Thou shalt not make a false statement or advance a false position.*

Does a person have a right to advance a position that is false, a common every-day occurrence in our society. It is done by people who are mistaken in their belief that a false position is true. And it is done by people who advance a position as true all the while knowing it to be false.

In discussing this then, the question arises of representing to others as true something that is false. This is a moral question. To phrase it another way does a person have a right to lie. And of course, in the case of a grievous matter, the answer is no. On the other hand there are circumstance in which this Precept may not apply such as in debate and meaningful communication.

We made the distinction of the exercise of this Precept within and without the parameters of meaningful communication. To repeat, we will hold that the right to hold a false position within the parameters of meaningful communication is valid for purposes of argument. And the right to hold a false position outside the parameters of meaningful communication may or may not be valid depending on circumstances.

In formal debate, a person may defend a position he knows to be false. Generally speaking, however, outside of debate, this Precept applies in all other areas such as advertising, politics, lawmaking and personal relations.

V. In dialogue the respondents have the obligation to correctly understand and accept the statement(s) and/or position(s) being advanced.

This precept corresponds to the Fifth Rule for Public Discourse: *Thou shalt not deliberately misrepresent any point of view.*

Everybody has the obligation to understand an opposing point of view and to represent it correctly.

Just as it is the obligation of the one communicating a position to make himself understood, it is the obligation of those receiving that communication to understand the position being communicated. Accepting a position as that of the person communicating it is a matter of acknowledgment and being fair minded. Agreement is not in question. If everyone has the right to his beliefs, everyone else has the obligation to acknowledge this.

But this precept also gives to the communicatee(s) the right to verify their understanding of what is being said.

All too often there are people who will not accept what they think is another person's position much less try to understand it.

If you are sincere in your desire to engage in meaningful communication, you will accept the position of the person advancing it. You will then want to understand it and you may do this by asking questions and making observations.

This does not mean you have to agree with the position being communicated. It just means you have to understand the communicator. It also means as a matter of courtesy that you should communicate back to the person advancing a position that you understand his position and that you accept it as his position. To do this you need to make sure that you really do understand his position by verifying it with him.

Everyone wants to be accepted. This is a basic desire of human nature. By assuring the one communicating a position that you understand and accept his position, you are in effect building a bridge of understanding with that person. You are, in a way, accepting him. This, in effect, has the potential to create a bond of friendship, which can produce an understanding much deeper than it otherwise would be and makes disagreements on positions much more palatable.

VI. Any person has a right to disagree with the position of any other person.

This precept corresponds to the Sixth Rule for Public Discourse, *Thou shalt acknowledge opposition statements*

This is a basic right and is obvious. Yet there are people who will not grant this right, so it needs to be stated. It is a corollary of the First Precept. If you have a right to your position and it disagrees with another person's position, then it follows that you have a right to disagree with that other position.

We need to distinguish between the exercise of this right within and without the parameters of meaningful communication. In meaningful communication we are generally concerned with impersonal ideas and coming to an agreement either on the points of disagreement or the truth or falsity of a position.

In philosophy the mantra of resolving a conflict is "distinguish and define." Whenever there is disagreement on a position, or between two or more positions, it is necessary to distinguish the points of disagreement and come to an agreement on the definition of the terms being used to define one or more positions.

Particular beliefs or positions can usually be summed up in a brief statement and as such can be analyzed and debated. In meaningful communication this must be kept on an impersonal level.

On a personal level this right can hit pretty close to home. People, as a rule, do not like to have their individual beliefs questioned by other people. There is an emotional element in finding fault with another person's beliefs and a corresponding defensive stance taken.

There are disagreements in all areas of human endeavor and a lot of conflict as a result. Because of the emotional element and problematic conflict, we need to take special care in challenging a position on which we disagree. In effect we need to rise above conflict and exercise a certain amount of tact.

In meaningful communication, the objective is to resolve conflict by reaching agreement either on the truth and validity of a position or on the points of disagreement.

VII All parties have the obligation to distinguish between a person and the position of that person.

This Precept corresponds to the Seventh Rule for Public Discourse: *Thou shalt distinguish between a person and his statement or argument.*

This Precept is much more applicable in the Rules for Public Discourse. To attack a person rather than his argument in constructive dialogue is much more obvious and unlikely to go unchallenged. It does have its violators in settings such as public hearings where the Rules for Public Discourse and Precepts of Dialogue overlap.

This of course is the fallacy argumentum ad hominem. A quick review of it is in the Seventh Rule for Public Discourse in Chapter IX. In dialogue, you never criticize the person, you criticize the position of that person.

A person's beliefs, life situations, history, or his character has nothing to do with the argument he makes or the stand that he takes. A questioner in a public hearing may call attention to a person's past or his affiliations in an attempt to discredit his testimony. This is a violation of the Seventh Rule for Public Discourse and the Seventh Precept of Dialogue.

VIII. All parties have the obligation to not impute to another person beliefs, knowledge, understanding, ignorance, feelings, thoughts, intentions, positions or any other thing.

This Precept corresponds to the Eighth Rule for Public Discourse: Thou *shalt not impute.*

The wording of the Rule and the Precept are identical and the explanation of this Precept is the same as that in Chapter X, "Explanation of Rules," and so will not be repeated here.

Imputing is a real obstacle to meaningful communication

Imputing is one of the most common and glaring mistakes made in all kinds of communications between two or more people. There is a tendency to judge other people by our beliefs and standards: what another person believes, what he has knowledge of, what he is ignorant of, his feelings, what he is thinking and what his intentions are.

This raises the specter of assumed accusations in which one person judges another on the basis of their own beliefs without taking into account that another person might have a different belief and as a result a different response to a specific act.

The fact is these kinds of judgments are likely to be wrong and are an obstacle to meaningful communication. There is no way that one person can know what is in another person's mind. So this precept requires us to accept what another person says about his position or any other thing. If a person wants to know, then the thing to do is ask.

IX. A negative universal statement may not be used in an argument or to make a point.

This Precept corresponds to the Ninth Rule for Public Discourse: *Thou shalt not use a negative universal statement in an argument or to make a point.*

As has previously been stated in a number of chapters, a negative universal statement is such that it generally cannot be proven and therefore cannot legitimately be made unless it is immediately obvious.

One should be on their guard for negative universal statements.

This rule is the subject of the most egregious violations by individuals in all walks of life including in academia and in politics. You can't prove that you can't prove something. The reasoning behind it is discussed in Chapter XII, "The Nature of Proof."

+X The person maintaining a position has a right to verify that all his statements and his position are correctly understood.

This precept (designated by a plus sign) is not included in the Rules For Public Discourse. It applies only to meaningful communication between two or more people about a specific subject.

This is one of the more important precepts and is not always obvious. If you are the one advancing a position, you will want to ascertain that your position is correctly understood. The usual way to do this is by asking questions and this precept gives the communicator the right to ask questions of the communicatees.

To reach agreement, the originator of a position may need to go to extraordinary lengths to make sure his position is understood. That is why, he has the right to establish the terms he is using to explain his position, which is the next Precept.

+XI. Any person maintaining a position has the right to promote it and the right and obligation to distinguish and define (within the rules of logic) the terms and concepts he uses.

This Precept is not included in the Rules For Public Discourse. It applies only to meaningful communication between two or more people about a specific subject.

This is different from the First Precept. The First Precept has to do with defining or explaining a position. This Eleventh Precept has to do with defining one or more terms and concepts used in explaining a position.

This Precept has major implications. We do not know what the other person knows or does not know, so we must take into account the level of intellection (knowledge) that the person or persons we are talking to has. If the dialogue we are having is with one or two other people, the Fifth Precept comes into play in which we are able to question their understanding of the position advocated. If we are not sure about another person's knowledge, we can verify his or her understanding by asking questions. In the case of a group, this is not practical. Therefore, it never hurts to assume that we need to provide elementary explanations because if we are talking to a group or addressing the universe, what seems simple to the communicator may be unknown or something else entirely to the communicatee(s).

Meaningful communication involves sending and receiving information in the form of mind data, which is represented by terms. Often this mind data, especially in philosophical discourse, consist of highly abstract concepts. This is often the case when a person is proposing a new theory or idea or position. And if a person has a right to his position, he not only has the right to make his position understood, but also the obligation to do so, if he is sincere.

The only way to create a new abstract concept is by definition and elaboration of that definition. In other words, the person advancing a new position does so by explaining what he means and this may even involve coining a new term or terms. Or it may involve using a traditional term in a new sense. Many of the terms used in computer science fit in this category. As we have seen in Chapter XI, there is much confusion on the use of words, terms and language.

There are those who will argue that you do not have the right to define the terms you use in advancing a position. They may disagree with your definition and therefore not accept it.

This attitude is the result of a failure to recognize and accept the *Principle of the Great Distinction*. That is they fail to recognize the distinction of the way things are in the mind and the spoken or written expression evidenced in the external world of the way things are in the mind. They fail to recognize how abstract concepts are communicated. They fail to recognize that for abstract concepts to be communicated they must be defined or explained.

Failure to recognize this is an out-of-hand rejection of an explanation and this results in an inability to receive the concept being communicated, and so raises an insurmountable obstacle to meaningful communication.

There is one major exception to this right. This right does not apply to the definition of truth. The definition of truth according to the correspondence concept must be adhered to for meaningful communication to be meaningful. There are all kinds of deception that can result by changing the definition of truth.

Another example of the establishment of this right is the way laws are written. In most instances, in the United States when the Congress, a state legislature or other political entity creates a new law, a part of that law is a definition of terms.

There has been much written on definitions of terms. The subject is a subdivision of logic. There are many kinds of definitions and there are many rules for creating definitions. They can be found in most textbooks on logic.

+XII. All those involved in constructive dialogue have the obligation to accept and use the terms and concepts as defined by the person advancing a position.

This precept is not included in the Rules For Public Discourse. It applies only to meaningful communication between two or more people about a specific subject.

This is also one of the more important precepts and follows from the Fifth Precept. In fact, as stated in the previous Precept, there will be many who will disagree with it. They may even argue against a position based on their definition of a term, which will be different than that of the person using it to explain his position.

You don't have the right to disagree with a definition of a term used by the person advancing a position. You have the obligation to understand his position. This is critical in many arguments. Often opposing sides in an argument are basing their support or opposition on different concepts they have of one or more terms being used. Simply put, if you are to understand another person's position, you must understand his explanation of it. To understand his explanation of it, you must understand and accept the terms he is using to explain it.

There are adherents who hold that terms are merely arbitrary and artificial symbols that we attach to things and have no relation to the way things are in reality. This is directly opposed to the great distinction and the correspondence theory of truth. Therefore, this is a false philosophy.

There are many such false philosophies. To know this, we do not have to know which is false and which is not. We can conclude from the principle of contradiction that two philosophical belief systems that disagree with each other cannot both be true representations of the way things are in reality. Most of philosophy consists of positions that do not agree with each other. So we can conclude that many philosophical positions are false. Which is true and which is false is not relevant to this conclusion. Based on the principle of contradiction we do not have to know which if any is true to reach this conclusion.

XIII All parties have the obligation to observe the rules of logic and identification of fallacies.

This Precept entails a basic understanding of certain elements of philosophy. There are many principles and axioms in philosophy.

In addition to these Precepts of Dialogue there are laws of thought, and principles and rules of logic, all of which apply to meaningful communication. These include rules for defining terms, rules for forming syllogisms and the identification of fallacies. These rules and fallacies are extensive and for most people, who master them, they involve a certain amount of formal education. A person need not be versed in all these rules and fallacies to engage in meaningful communication. However, a person needs to understand that they exist and to acknowledge that they are valid when confronted with them.

Among the principles of logic are certain commandments of reason which we will label Precepts of Discernment.

PRECEPTS OF DISCERNMENT

Precepts of discernment that helpful in determining the truth or falsity of a statement and what to believe and not believe about all statements. They are:

- **Do not accept as true anything that has not been proven to be true.**

- **Distinguish fact from opinion**

- **Do not unreasonably disregard anything that has not been disproved.**

- **Always distinguish between the way things are in external reality and the way things are in the mind.**

- **Never argue about established facts.**

- Accept what is true.

- Reject what is false.

- Withhold judgment on everything else.

- To resolve disagreements always distinguish and define positions and terms

CHAPTER XVII
APPLICATION OF PRECEPTS

There is no authority to which one might appeal when someone violates the rules of civility, the Rules for Public Discourse and the Precepts of Dialogue. There is however the voice of the people which can have a powerful effect on politicians and the press. Thanks to social media people are empowered in ways never seen before. Tunisia, Libya and Egypt are striking examples of it.

Probably, there are politicians, public officials and others who violate the Rules and Precepts laid down here unintentionally through ignorance or happenstance. These people need to be educated or alerted to their violation. Many who have made statements in violation of the Rules and Precepts laid down here, will acknowledge their mistake and try to avoid making the same mistake again.

On the other hand, there may be those in Congress and the media who have a disdain for these Rules and Precepts and violate them continually with impunity. These people need to be upbraided and held up as lacking integrity.

The Rules and Precepts set forth herein can be powerful tools when referenced in an email or a tweet and/or held up on Facebook, or Utube and other similar sites. The mere statement when you address someone and say, "You are violating the Rules for Public Discourse when you (here state the violation)" lends credence to your complaint.

The precepts of dialogue offer tools that can be used to get a point across and further constructive discourse. They really work if they are used correctly and skillfully. To really use them, they must be always available.

Occasions will arise in which one can redirect a conversation in a constructive manner. This is what each of the precepts can do. For example, one common violation is the accusing of another person of wrongful feelings or beliefs or lack of knowledge. It is a simple matter to point out that the person making the accusation does not know what another person's feelings or beliefs are or what another person knows or doesn't know. Pointing out the imputing can be reinforced if one knows the specific rule in question and can say, "that is a violation of the Eighth Rule for Public Discourse" if you are holding someone accountable, or the "Eighth Precept of Dialogue" if you are involved in meaningful communication.

This same tactic can be applied with all the Rules for Public Discourse and the Precepts of Dialogue.

The rules of civility are of a little different genre than the Rules for Public Discourse and the Precepts of Dialogue. There are people with good manners and there are people with bad manners and it is often not very tactful to call a person to task over his manners. Still making the point that "being civil can be helpful in solving problems," can be helpful in solving problems. And the rules of civility can be most useful in alerting ourselves to our own shortcomings.

Citing rules has a certain force. An example occurred on November 7, 2011 during an encounter of Herman Cain with the press when he was twice asked about sexual harassment. Cain said he would not go there. When asked about it again Cain asked his chief of staff to supply the questioner "with the Journalistic Code of Ethics," which had the desired effect of putting the damper on the pursuit of that particular issue.

There are a number of codes promulgated by different organizations. Interestingly, a purview of the various codes did not reveal any rule that addressed continued questioning of a candidate against his wishes about a subject he refused to talk about.[1]

APPENDIX A
EPILOGUE

We accept the fact that few people are interested in reigning in political rhetoric. Fewer still are interested in the Rules for Public Discourse. It is a sad commentary on American politics and the truism that people get the kind of government they deserve.

So why bother? Why joust at windmills? There are several reasons. The first is that there really does need to be a standard even if it is totally ignored and/or does not receive any official recognition as such. The second is that this book is much more than just about rules for public discourse. It is also about truth and resolving disagreements. The "Precepts of Dialogue" at the end of the book can enrich anyone's life who reads, studies and uses them.

What may appear as bias against the Republicans is really the circumstance that it is the Republicans who were most in the news during the compiling of this book. The Republicans controlled the House and it is Republicans who were doing battle for their party's nomination for president. We can't control the fact that during the compiling of this book nearly all the news was about Republicans and very little was about Democrats. We will continue compiling violations of the Rules for Public Discourse without regard to which Party makes them. Anyone wishing to assist us in compiling violations may do so at wrii.org/RFPD.

As for philosophy, it has been a life-long passion of mine, enhanced by formal graduate studies and a lot of research. Anyone can be in error. If I have erred in any way in any part of this book, I am receptive to, even eager for, any demonstration to the contrary of what I have written. Reality is a tenuous thing from the perception point of view. I don't claim any special expertise or any remarkable insight. What has been set down here, has been written from the point of view of common sense.

Anyone has a right to dispute what I have said. If I can be shown the error of my ways, I will correct them.

The philosophy propounded here is philosophy in the traditional sense. It is somewhat at odds with the analytic philosophy that holds sway in most of today's universities. It is in accord with the philosophy of Mortimer Adler, an outspoken critic of analytic philosophy.

I really am a humble seeker after truth and will be happy to enter into constructive dialogue with anyone who wishes to do so as long as the Precepts of Dialogue are observed. My email address as of this writing is hoppins@earthlink.net

Charles Hoppins
December 2011

Nimis quidpiam serio non aspice

APPENDIX B
END NOTES

PREFACE

1. The Rules for Public Discourse are original. They were adapted from the Ten Precepts of Dialogue, which also were original. Ten Precepts of Dialogue was first published in 1997 in a book entitled The Way Things Are, The Basic Precepts of Reality and Common Sense (Hoppins, C., Boise ID: Western Research Press).

Rules and precepts are used in two senses. Rules and precepts that are used in the generic sense are not capitalized. When referring to one or all of the Rules for Public Discourse listed in Chapter VII and the Precepts of Dialogue listed in Chapter XVI, they are capitalized.

INTRODUCTION

1. There are two unreasonable positions involved in solving the deficit and debt crisis. One is that it can be done without raising revenue. The other is that it can be done without reforming Medicare and Medicaid.

2. This poll, which asked "What is truth?" has a long history. At first the results were not recorded. When it became evident that nearly every answer was different, the author began recording the answers under the auspices of Western Research Institute. Still it was very informal until 2010, when the results of it became an important element in Book Two in The Way Things Are series and we realized that this was a very difficult question for people to answer and further questioning was usually needed to determine people's true perception of what truth is.

At the beginning of 2011, we added the question "What makes a thing or statement true?" and set up a web site whereby we could classify the respondents as to gender, age, occupation, education level and political viewpoint. As of this writing this Web site was at irsonline.org.

3. This quote was taken from a speech Adler made in 1961 to "Members of the Million-Dollar Round Table," an association of life insurance agents. Adler indicated in his speech that his position at the time was "Director of the Institute for Philosophical Research in San Francisco."

Adler (1902-2001) reached celebrity status with the publication in 1952 of the 54 volume set of the Great Books of the Western World by Encyclopedia Britannica, which he co-edited with Robert M. Hutchins. He was greatly influenced by the philosophy of Aristotle and Thomas Aquinas and authored many books on philosophy and education. His philosophy supports the traditional basic philosophy espoused in this book.

CHAPTER I, IS WASHINGTON BROKEN?

1. Many professions have rules or guidelines that govern conduct within each profession including legal, accounting, journalism, medical etc. For rules governing journalists see Endnote #1 under Chapter XVII, "Application of Rules."

2.Rules of civility are discussed in Chapter XVI.

3.. Precepts of Dialogue are discussed in Chapter XVII.

4.. There are many kinds of debate and parliamentary settings, each with their own rules.

5.. van Eemeren, F. R. Grootendorst and F.S. Henemans (2002), Argumentation, Analysis, Evaluation, Presentation, Mahwah, NJ: Lawrence Erlbaum Associates, Inc. The book lists "10 Rules for Critical Discussion."

6.. Trading on insider information is punishable by stiff penalties. Members of Congress have for many years exempted themselves from this law. Due to pressure from the media, legislation eliminating the exemption for members of Congress was passed in 2012.

CHAPTER II, WHAT IS INTEGRITY

1. Extreme positions include that budget deficits and the huge burden of public debt can be resolved with no new revenue on the one hand and that it can be resolved without modifying Medicare and Medicaid on the other hand.

CHAPTER III, THE CURRENT CLIMATE

1. Grover Norquist is founder and president of Americans for Tax Reform (atr.org). It's Web site lists all the 41 Senators and 238 representatives in the 112th Congress who have signed Norquist's no new taxes pledge.

2. Web sites that claim to represent the **Tea Party** include TeaParty.org, theteaparty.net, teapartyexpress.org. and the teapartynation.com. The Tea Party Express claims it has become the most aggressive and influential national Tea Party group in the political arena." **The Tea Party Express** says it stands for six simple principles:

- No more bailouts
- Reduce the size and intrusiveness of government
- Stop raising our taxes
- Repeal Obamacare
- Cease out-of-control spending
- Bring back American prosperity

The Tea Party Nation Pledge is, I will:

- Vote against and oppose any increase in taxes.
- Vote against and oppose any effort to balance the budget…by borrowing money.
- Vote for and support a balanced budget…through normal revenues.
- Within one year of the election, I will vote for…a measure to reduce government spending…by at least 10%.

The Tea Party Patriots (teapartypatriots.org) claims it is the largest tea party organization in the country. It says it "exists to serve and support the thousands of local organizations…"

3. Her Web site is at bachmann.house.gov.

4. The two Democratic House members who signed the pledge were Robert Andrews of New Jersey and Ben Chandler of Kentucky. Ben Nelson of Nebraska was the loan Democratic senator who signed the pledge.

5. The seven GOP senators who did not sign the pledge were Richard Lugar of Indiana; Charles Grassley of Iowa, Olympia Snowe and Susan Collins of Maine; John Barrasso of Wyoming and John Hoeven of North Dakota.

The six GOP House members who did not sign the pledge were Richard Hanna of New York, Rob Woodall of Georgia, Todd Russell Platts of Pennsylvania, Rob Whitman and Frank Wolf of Virginia, and Kevin Yoder of Kansas.

CHAPTER V, THE PRACTICE OF DECEPTION

1. De Sophisticis Elenchis (On Sophistical Refutations) There are translations of Aristotle's works available in book stores and at online book sellers.

2. One of the best sites on the Internet that covers the subject of fallacies as of 2011 is fallacyfiles.org. It lists some 160 different kinds of fallacies and examples.

3. Huckabee's remarks on Fox News and a radio talk show that Obama grew up in Kenya got him noticed and excoriated by major news outlets in the U.S. and U.K.

CHAPTER VI, COMMUNICATION AND RHETORIC

1. See Chapter I, Notes 1 to 5.

CHAPTER VIII, THE ROLE OF PHILOSOPHY

1. These statements reflect the sentiments formed from informal interviews in polling by the author and are a matter of opinion.

2. There is a position in analytic philosophy that holds there is no such thing as a basic philosophy. This is a negative universal, which cannot be proven. It can however be disproved. That is, it can be proven to be false by using the principle of contradiction, which we just did. The principle of contradiction is the most basic principle of basic philosophy, which Aristotle held.

CHAPTER IX, EXPLANATION OF RULES

1. These are all unsubstantiated statements. In addition they are negative universal statements, all of which cannot be proven. In the matter of Gingrich's baggage, this was a claim made in a number of negative super PAC advertisements in support of Mitt Romney. The ads were attributed to Gingrich losing much of his support in the Iowa Caucuses.

2. Solyndra was a solar panel manufacturer based in Fremont, California. The Obama administration authorized a half-billion dollar loan guarantee and touted the company as an example of its job growth stimulus program. The company filed for Chapter 11 bankruptcy in September, 2011.

Fast and Furious was an operation of the Bureau of Alcohol, Tobacco and Firearms in which the Bureau encouraged gun dealers to sell multiple weapons to purchasers so they could track the weapons to drug cartels in Mexico. The operation fell apart and the ATF lost track of the guns, one of which killed a border patrol agent.

3. All the presidential candidates have probably made false statements. We say "some" presidential candidates because we do not have documentation on all the candidates as of this writing..

4. Like the note above, we say "some" because we do not have documentation on all the candidates.

CHAPTER X, WHAT IS TRUTH

1. See poll, Endnote #1 under "Introduction."

2. Muggeridge, M., (1980), The End of Christianity, Grand Rapids MI: William B. Eerdsman Publishing Co. Muggeridge was a renowned English journalist, a radio and television personality and editor of Punch,

the English humor magazine. He discussed the tragedy of losing the meaning of words in the above book.

3. The current poll (as of this writing) was at irsonline.org.

4. This was written by Saikat Guha (1976-2008), a brilliant graduate student at University of Washington and Syracuse University. It was excerpted from a paper entitled, "The One: A Defense of Monism." It can be found along with other works by Guha at saikatguha.com.

CHAPTER XIV, THE PRESS AND THE MEDIA

1. This is a violation of the Fifth Rule for Public Discourse, *Thou shalt not deliberately misrepresent any point of view.*

CHAPTER XV, OTHER RULES

1. Again, when speaking generally of rules and precepts, they are not capitalized. When speaking of the specific Rules and Precepts listed here, they are capitalized.

2. Many various editions of the book are still being offered for sale. The book first came out in 1922.

3. A list of the rules can also be found on the Web site of National Public Radio at npr.org and typing in "George Washington Rules of Civility." There are also other books that deal with civility.

CHAPTER XVI, PRECEPTS OF DIALOGUE

1. One such is the National Coalition for Dialogue and Deliberation (NCDD). It's web site is at thataway.org. Tom Atlee has some interesting alternative perspectives on dialogue and where it can lead. His web site is at co-intelligence.org.

CHAPTER XVII, APPLICATION OF RULES

1. There are a number of news organizations which maintain "codes of ethics." These include Society of Professional Journalists, Code of Ethics, (spj.org/ethicscode.asp); Associated Press Managing Editors, Statement of Ethical Principles, (apme.com); and American Society of Newspaper Editors, Statement of Principles(asne.org).

APPENDIX C
REFERENCES

Adler, M.J., (1985) *Ten Philosophical Mistakes*, New York: Simon & Schuster.

Adler, M.J. and C. Van Doren (1972), *How to Read A Book*, New York: MJF Books.

Audi, R., ed. (1999), *Cambridge Dictionary of Philosophy*, 2nd edition, Cambridge, U.K: Cambridge University Press.

Boundas, C., ed. (2007), *Columbia Companion to Twentieth-Century Philosophies*, New York: Columbia University Press.

Copi, I.M., (1986) [2002] *Introduction to Logic*, New York: MacMillan Publishing Company.

van Eemeren, F., R. Grootendorst and F.S. Henemans (2002), *Argumentation, Analysis, Evaluation, Presentation*, Mahwah, NJ: Lawrence Erlbaum Associates, Inc.

Lepore, J., (2010) *The Whites of Their Eyes, The Tea Party's Revolution and the Battle Over American History*, Princeton, NJ: Princeton University Press.

Loewen, J.L., (2007) [1995], *Lies My Teacher Told Me*, New York: Simon & Schuster, Inc.

Groothuis, D., (2000), *Truth Decay, Defending Christianity Against the Challenges of Postmodernism*, Downers Grove IL: InterVarsity Press.

MUGGERIDGE, M., (1980), *The End of Christianity,* Grand Rapids MI: William B. Eerdsman Publishing Co.

Perelman, C. and L. Olbrechts-Tyteca, (1969) *The New Rhetoric, A Treatise on Argumentation*, Notre Dame IN: Notre Dame University Press.

Walton, D., (2006*), Fundamentals of Critical Argumentation*, New York: Cambridge University Press.

Weston, A. (2009), *A Rule Book for Arguments*, Indianapolis, IN: Hackett Publishing Co.

APPENDIX F
WESTERN RESEARCH
(Since 1987)

This book was compiled and published under the auspices of Western Research Institute (WRI). WRI is a non-profit Idaho corporation serving the general public, private clients, the press and government. The main purpose for which WRI was founded, was and still is, investigations and reporting. The Institute is first of all a provider of facts. Most of what the Institute does is centered on this mission. Facts compiled are issued in the form of reports or books.

In addition to compiling and publishing reports and books, WRI is involved in the collection and dissemination of news and opinion with special emphasis on the law, the courts and the legal profession. WRI is an independent non-partisan reporter of facts. It has no agenda except freedom of information and holding public officials and others accountable for what they say for public consumption.

WRI has compiled and published a number of reports and books on various subjects including law, government, technology, philosophy and communication.

Its main mission remains serving the public and the press with information that would otherwise not see the light of day. Only a tiny fraction of the events in this country and around the world are ever reported on. Very little activity of what transpires in the myriad of government agencies in this country ever reaches the public eye.

WRI was incorporated in January of 1987 and has been in continuous existence since then. This can be verified by clicking on the business entities section of the Idaho Secretary of State. Further information is at the WRI web site at wrii.org. (The full URL is wikiwacky.net/wrii.)

APPENDIX E
ABOUT THE AUTHOR

Charles Hoppins is a semi-retired journalist with a passion for philosophy enhanced by formal graduate study and a lot of research. He has worked for The Associated Press and a number of newspapers as writer, assistant city editor, state editor and wire editor.

Reporters working for news organizations are under constant pressure to produce copy and meet deadlines. The stories they cover often have serious ramifications that are dealt with only on a superficial basis. Troubled by the lack of time to do serious in depth reporting on a number of stories, he conceived of the idea of a research institution that would have the funding and ability to cover stories that would otherwise not see the light of day.

In 1987, he was a principle in the founding of Western Research Institute (WRI). From its inception WRI set out to do in-depth reporting on a number of issues. It has done reports and published books on technology, law, government, philosophy and communication.

For the past number of years he has been involved in the study of the prevalence of certain philosophical positions and how those positions affect society, human behavior and public policy. He has completed a number of books on the results, the last involving precepts of dialogue and general principles of communication.

The outcome of these studies, is the publication of *Rules for Public Discourse*, on how to hold lawmakers, candidates for public office and others accountable for what they say for public consumption.

As part of WRI's commitment to public interest research, he has in collaboration with Jerry Fenning embarked on an in-depth research project involving reports on *How America Can Stop Importing Foreign Oil* and *The Fight Over Using Natural Gas for Transportaion..*

How America Can Stop Importing Foreign Oil is available in a print edition and an ebook edition. The ebook edition is available on Kindle, Nook, Smashwords.com and Apple and Google devices.

APPENDIX F
EASY REFERENCE TEAR-OUT PAGE
RULES FOR PUBLIC DISCOURSE

I. Thou shalt not prevent anyone from speaking out.

II. Thou shalt not evade a question by addressing another issue or by responding to a question with a question.

III. Thou shalt not make unsubstantiated claims.

IV. Thou shalt not make a false statement or advance a false position.

V. Thou shalt not deliberately misrepresent any point of view.

VI. Thou shalt acknowledge opposition statements.

VII. Thou shalt distinguish between a person and the statement or argument of that person.

VIII. Thou shalt not impute.

IX. Thou shalt not use a negative universal statement in an argument or an assertion.

X. Thou shalt not use fallacious or illogical arguments.

PRECEPTS OF DIALOGUE

I. Everybody has a right to his position

II. In dialogue, the respondents have the obligation to address the issued being advanced.

III. Anyone making a claim must substantiate it.

IV. No one has the right to advance a false statement or position.

V. In dialogue the respondents have the obligation to correctly understand everything.

VI. Any person has a right to disagree with the position of any other person.

VII. All parties have the obligation to distinguish between a person and the position of that person.

VIII.. All parties have the obligation to not impute.

IX. A negative universal statement may not be used in an argument or to make a point.

+X. The proponent of a statement or position has a right to verify that his statements and his position are correctly understood.

+XI. The proponent of a position has obligation to distinguish and define (within the rules of logic) the terms and concepts he uses.

+XII. All those involved in constructive dialogue have the obligation to accept and use the terms and concepts as defined by the person advancing a position.

XIII. All parties have the obligation to observe the rules of logic and identification of fallacies.

www.ingramcontent.com/pod-product-compliance
Lightning Source LLC
Chambersburg PA
CBHW031208270326
41931CB00006B/469